YEAR A
ADVENT/CHRISTMAS/EPIPHANY

YEAR A
ADVENT/CHRISTMAS/EPIPHANY

PREACHING
THE REVISED
COMMON
LECTIONARY

Marion Soards
Thomas Dozeman
Kendall McCabe

ABINGDON PRESS
Nashville

Preaching the Revised Common Lectionary
Year a: Advent, Christmas, Epiphany

This book is printed on recycled, acid-free paper.

Library of Congress Cataloging-in-Publication Data

Soards, Marion L., 1952–
     Preaching the revised Common lectionary: year A/Marion L. Soards, Thomas B.
Dozeman, Kendall McCabe.
     p. cm.
     Includes indexes.
     [1] Advent, Christmas, Epiphany— [2] Lent and Easter.
     ISBN 0-687-33800-X (v. 1: alk. paper)—ISBN 0-687-33801-8 Iv. 2: alk. paper)

     1. Bible—Liturgical lessons, English. 2. Bible—Homiletical use.
I. Dozeman, Thomas B. II. McCabe, Kendall, 1939–   . III. Title.
BS 391.2.S59   1992
251—dc20   91-34039
                                                                      CIP

You may order the software edition of *Preaching the Revised Common Lectionary,*
packaged in Year A, B, or C, from your local religious bookstore, or by calling
1-800-672-1789. Specify whether your computer system is running at least DOS 3.0
or Windows.

95 96 97 98 99 00 01 — 10 9 8 7 6 5 4

MANUFACTURED IN THE UNITED STATES OF AMERICA

Contents

CONTENTS

This is one volume in a twelve-volume series. Each volume contains commentary and worship suggestions for a portion of lectionary cycle A, B, or C. Since the lections for a few special days do not change from one lectionary cycle to another, material for each of these days appears in only one of the volumes. Appropriate cross references in the table of contents lead the reader to material in other volumes of the series.

Introduction

Now pastors and students have a systematic treatment of essential issues of the Christian year and Bible study for worship and proclamation based on the Revised Common Lectionary. Interpretation of the lectionary will separate into three parts: Calendar, Canon, and Celebration. A brief word of introduction will provide helpful guidelines for utilizing this resource in worship through the Christian year.

Calendar. Every season of the Christian year will be introduced with a theological interpretation of its meaning, and how it relates to the overall Christian year. This section will also include specific liturgical suggestions for the season.

Canon. The lectionary passages will be interpreted in terms of their setting, structure, and significance. First, the word *setting* is being used loosely in this commentary to include a range of different contexts in which biblical texts can be interpreted from literary setting to historical or cultic settings. Second, regardless of how the text is approached under the heading of setting, interpretation will always proceed to an analysis of the structure of the text under study. Third, under the heading of significance, central themes and motifs of the passage will be underscored to provide a theological interpretation of the text as a springboard for preaching. Thus interpretation of the lectionary passages will result in the outline on the next page.

Celebration. This section will focus on specific ways of relating the lessons to liturgical acts and/or homiletical options for the day on which they occur. How the texts have been used in the Christian tradition will sometimes be illustrated to stimulate the thinking of preachers and planners of worship services.

I. OLD TESTAMENT TEXTS

A. The Old Testament Lesson

1. Setting

2. Structure

3. Significance

B. Psalm

1. Setting

2. Structure

3. Significance

II. NEW TESTAMENT TEXTS

A. The Epistle

1. Setting

2. Structure

3. Significance

B. The Gospel

1. Setting

2. Structure

3. Significance

Why We Use the Lectionary

Although many denominations have been officially or unofficially using some form of the lectionary for many years some pastors are still unclear about where it comes from, why some lectionaries differ from denomination to denomination, and why the use of a lectionary is to be preferred to a more random sampling of scripture.

Simply put, the use of a lectionary provides a more diverse scriptural diet for God's people, and it can help protect the congregation from the whims and prejudices of the pastor and other worship planners. Faithful use of the lectionary means that preachers must deal with texts they would rather ignore, but about which the congregation may have great concern and interest. An apocalyptic text, such as we encounter in this volume on the First Sunday of Advent, might be a case in point. Adherence to the lectionary can be an antidote to that homiletical arrogance that says, "I know what my people need," and in humility acknowledges that the Word of God found in scripture may speak to more needs on Sunday morning than we even know exist, when we seek to proclaim faithfully the message we have wrestled from the text.

The lectionary may also serve as a resource for liturgical content. The psalm is intended to be a response to the Old Testament lesson, and not read as a lesson itself, but beyond that the lessons may inform the content of prayers of confession, intercession, and petition. Some lessons may be adapted as affirmations of faith, as in *The United Methodist Hymnal,* nos. 887-889; the United Church of Christ's *Hymnal,* nos. 429-430; and the Presbyterian *Worshipbook,* no. 30. The "Celebration" entries for each day will call attention to these opportunities from time to time.

Pastors and preachers in the free-church tradition should think of the lectionary as a primary resource for preaching and worship, but

9

need to remember that the lectionary was made for them and not they for the lectionary. The lectionary may serve as the inspiration for a separate series of lessons and sermons that will include texts not in the present edition, or having chosen one of the lectionary passages as the basis for the day's sermon, the preacher may wish to make an independent choice of the other lessons to supplement and illustrate the primary text. The lectionary will be of most value when its use is not a cause for legalism but for inspiration.

Just as there are no perfect preachers, there are no perfect lectionaries. The Revised Common Lectionary, upon which this series is based, is the result of the work of many years by the Consultation on Common Texts and is a response to ongoing evaluation of the *Common Lectionary* (1983) by pastors and scholars from the several participating denominations. The current interest in the lectionary can be traced back to the Second Vatican Council, which ordered lectionary revision for the Roman Catholic Church:

> The treasures of the Bible are to be opened up more lavishly, so that richer fare may be provided for the faithful at the table of God's Word. In this way a more representative portion of the holy Scriptures will be read to the people over a set cycle of years. (*The Documents of Vatican II*, Walter Abbott, ed. [Piscataway, N.J.: New Century, 1974], p. 155)

The example thus set by Roman Catholics inspired Protestants to take more seriously the place of the Bible in their services and sermons, and soon many denominations had issued their own three-year cycles, based generally on the Roman Catholic model but with their own modifications. This explains why some discrepancies and variations appear in different forms of the lectionary. The Revised Common Lectionary (RCL) is an effort to increase agreement among the churches. A table at the end of the volume will list the differences between the RCL and the Roman Catholic, Episcopal, and Lutheran lectionaries. Where no entry is made, all are in agreement with the RCL.

For those unacquainted with the general pattern of the lectionary, a brief word of explanation may be helpful for sermon preparation. (1) The three years are each distinguished by one of the Synoptic Gospels: Matthew in A, Mark in B, Luke in C. John is distributed over the three years with a heavy emphasis during Lent and Easter. (2) Two types of readings are used. During the periods of Advent to Epiphany and Lent to Pentecost, the readings are usually topical, that is, there is some common theme among them. During the Sundays after Epiphany and Pentecost the readings are continuous, with no necessary connection between the lessons. In the period covered by this volume (Advent, Christmas, Epiphany), there is a thematic connection between the Old Testament lesson and the Gospel during the Sundays after Epiphany, but the epistle lesson begins a continuous reading from I Corinthians. The preacher begins, then, with at least four preaching options: to deal with either one of the lessons on its own or to work with the dialogue between the Old Testament lesson and the Gospel. Perhaps it should also be added that though the psalm is intended to be a response by the people to the Old Testament lesson—rather than as a lesson on its own—this in no way suggests that it cannot be used as the text for the sermon.

This is the first of four volumes that will deal with the lessons for the entire A Cycle of the Christian year. Volume 2 will include Ash Wednesday through the Day of Pentecost. Volume 3 begins with Trinity Sunday (the First Sunday After Pentecost) and includes all the lessons for June, July, and August. Volume 4 finishes the remainder of the year, including the lessons for All Saints' Day (November 1). A new series will then be published for the B Cycle.

A note on language: We have used the term *Old Testament* in this series because that is the language employed by the Consultation on Common Texts, at least up to this point. Pastors and worship committees may wish to consider alternative terms, such as *First Testament* or *Hebrew Scriptures*, that do not imply that those writings somehow have less value than the rest of the Christian Bible. Another option is to refer to *First Lesson* (always from the Hebrew Scriptures), *Second Lesson* (from Acts or the epistles), and *Gospel*.

THE PASCHAL MYSTERY AND ADVENT

Preachers and liturgical planners who seek to take seriously the Christian year as the basis of their work need to remember first of all that the purpose for the year is to allow us to focus on particular aspects of the Easter proclamation and their relevance to Christian life and thought. Easter is at the center of the Christian faith; without Easter there could be no Christian faith, only the Good Friday memory of a man who tried valiantly to make a witness about God and failed. The Christian year grew out of the Church's desire to participate as fully as possible in every aspect of the Paschal mystery by dynamically remembering and thus sharing in the salvation-giving events recorded in scripture.

Thus understood, the observance of the Christian year is not the same as the annual cyclical celebrations of the Greco-Roman mystery religions. In the mystery religions, the gods needed to have the ritual activities performed in order to assist them in bringing about the salvation of the performers; the gods were dependent upon the worshipers for their very existence. It was the activity of the faithful that brought the god back to life. In Christian worship, we acknowledge what God has done and is doing by virtue of God's own will and power. So for Christians, the Resurrection is a fact proclaimed and experienced, rather than a need of God that the worshiper is called upon to help bring about. God is responsible for the Easter triumph, not us or even our faith in the Resurrection.

This means that the Church does not approach Advent pretending that Jesus has not yet been born or that we know nothing about Calvary and the empty tomb. Advent is celebrated in the light of the Christ-event; it is an examination and celebration of the Easter mystery from this side of the empty tomb. We do not sing Christmas carols or preach sermon series on "They Met at the Manger" during

Advent because we are ignorant of Christmas, but because we wish to experience and proclaim that hope which in Israel waited in faith for the Messiah during the darkest and most desolate of times, and which since Easter still waits "for the revealing of our Lord Jesus Christ" (I Cor. 1:7, Second Reading, First Sunday of Advent, Year B).

Advent is the Janus of the Christian year. It looks backward at Israel's expectation of a Messiah (the Old Testament lessons), and it looks forward to the consummation, to the ultimate triumph of Christ over the power of sin and death that was begun on that first Easter Day. Advent, in its message of judgment and the reign of Christ, is as much a result of Easter as it is an anticipation of Easter and may be considered the end of the Christian year as appropriately as it is considered the beginning. Because we mortals are linear beings, creatures of time, we usually want things to have a beginning and an end. Because Advent does deal with the expectation of the Messiah and the preparations for his birth, there is a logic in using it to begin the annual cycle.

Once again, we must remember that this is not a cyclic event as in the mystery religions, where the god is dependent upon our actions for his or her existence and where the same event occurs over and over again. We may use the term *cycle* as a matter of convenience, but the fact is that we are not the same persons who celebrated Advent last year, and we are not the same persons who will celebrate Advent next year. Yearly we bring another 365 days of grace to our celebration, and so our insight into the paschal mystery is deeper and our observance conditioned by the previous year's "dangers, toils, and fears." We are not the same people doing the same thing year after year. The hope we bring to this year's Advent is not the same hope we brought last year, for it has been tempered and informed by "the encouragement of the scriptures" (Romans 15:4, Second Reading, Second Sunday of Advent, Year A), as during the year we have sought to "put on the Lord Jesus Christ" (Romans 13:14, Second Reading, First Sunday of Advent, Year A).

The Liturgical Environment

Colors. Purple has been the customary color for Advent in the Western Church since the sixteenth century. There has been a recent trend to the use of blue, based on the inventories of some medieval churches. Rigidity over the use of color did not come about until the Reformation, when the invention of printing allowed everything to be rubricized and regulated. The catalogs of publishing houses notwithstanding, purple is not primarily a color of penitence; that is a symbolism attached to the color after the fact, once purple had been assigned to Lent and then to Advent. The penitential character of Lent gave symbolic interpretation to the color. In the ancient world, purple was the color of royalty, since only a royal income could afford the dye that made it possible. Purple, then, points to the kingship of Christ, "the Lord's anointed, great David's greater Son." We decorate our churches in purple or royal blue (not a pastel blue) to prepare for the coming of the King.

The use of a pink candle in the Advent wreath is an imitation of a Roman Catholic practice that is not even required of churches outside the city of Rome itself. The observance of Lent/Easter is older than that of Advent/Christmas, and so the liturgical practices of Advent tended to be modeled on those that had developed earlier for Lent. An idiosyncracy in the Roman practice developed because by the early Middle Ages the custom had developed for the pope, as a sign of special favor, to give a golden rose to persons he especially esteemed. He did this on the Fourth Sunday in Lent, and in honor of the occasion the churches were decorated with rose-colored paraments. The day came to be seen as a respite before plunging into the rigors of the last days of the Lenten fast. It also helped that the first word of the introit for that Sunday was "laetare," rejoice. Because Advent was looked upon as a "little Lent," it became the custom on the third Sunday (when the first word of the introit was "gaudete," also "rejoice") to use rose vestments to parallel the Lenten pattern.

Advent wreaths. Advent wreaths have become popular visual aids in many churches to mark the time through Advent, and the making of them provides activities for the church school, family nights, and similar meetings. Often the products are then used as a part of individual or family devotions throughout the season. Family units are often employed to do the lighting of the wreath at the beginning of the church service each Sunday. (Pastors might want to examine what kind of silent judgment this pronounces against single persons. Is it a reinforcement of the popular myth that "Christmas is only for children" or that the season can only be appreciated in a family context?)

Please note that the various candles on the Advent wreath don't mean anything! To paraphrase Archibald MacLeish's comment on poetry, "An Advent wreath should not mean, but be." Symbolization, the attribution of one meaning to a thing that does not in itself evoke that meaning, is a frequent liturgical error; we inhibit or restrict meaning by insisting that things should mean only the one thing we arbitrarily assign to them. If individuals or groups are going to prepare their own liturgies for the lighting of the wreath, and insist on attributing meaning to each candle, then the meaning (or more accurately, the theme) should grow out of a consideration of the lessons for the day, and that theme may appropriately change from year to year.

Chrismons. A more recent appearance has been made in many churches by chrismon trees hung with symbols of Christ. It is difficult to avoid the suspicion that these are a means of sneaking Christmas trees onto the scene early. If they are to be used at all, they certainly should not be evergreens. It would be preferable to use something of bare branches only. Following the same logic, the hanging of the greens is inappropriate before the Fourth Sunday of Advent, no matter how close to Christmas itself that may be. The absence of any altar flowers during these four Sundays can be a remarkable contrast to the explosion of poinsettias that is to come.

Silence. Advent is a time to encourage the use of silence. Waiting and watching are major themes of the season, and they can be reinforced by ritual silence that should stand in marked contrast to the musical merriment of the Christmas celebration. Roman Catholic, Lutheran, and Anglican churches have customarily suppressed the use of the *Gloria in excelsis Deo* ("Glory be to God on high") during Advent, so that this song of the angels is heard with a fresh appreciation at the first service of Christmas. An absence of organ voluntaries may also be appropriate.

A hymn. The hymn "O Come, O Come, Emmanuel" and the "O" antiphons on which it is based provide a number of significant images for use as Advent visuals on bulletins, paraments, vestments, and so on. (Different versions include no. 211 in *The United Methodist Hymnal*; no. 56 in the Episcopal *The Hymnal, 1982*; and pages 174-75 in *The Lutheran Book of Worship*.) Among them are a crown and scepter for the expected king, a key, a star of David, a Jesse tree, and a rising sun. The application of the title "Wisdom" (Sophia or Sapientia) to Christ in the text of "O Come, O Come, Emmanuel" reminds us of the sexual inclusiveness of redemption since Wisdom has often been portrayed as a female. This use is also found in the hymn "O Word of God Incarnate." The thoughtful pastor might wish to relate these images to the New Testament lesson for the Second Sunday of Advent in year A with its reference to the scriptures. It was because this lesson was the standard one in the old lectionary that for many years the second Sunday in December (frequently the second of Advent) was celebrated as Bible Sunday. Cranmer's collect, "Blessed Lord, who hast caused all holy scriptures to be written for our learning," was composed for the Second Sunday of Advent. Bible Sunday is now officially the Sunday before Thanksgiving Day, which doesn't give it any better chance of recognition than it had before, so this Sunday in year A might still serve as a time to emphasize in some way the scriptures as the cradle which holds the Incarnate Word, as the pulpit through which the apostles continue to proclaim what they saw and heard. Christ as Wisdom extends beyond the image of the Bible alone, and worship planners are challenged to think of other visual and symbolic expressions that may be employed.

Because "O Come, O Come, Emmanuel" is so rich with images, its use ought not be restricted to once during the season (particularly now that many hymnals include seven rather than four stanzas). The stanzas might be divided among the Sundays and used as a part of the lighting of the Advent wreath or some other act of worship. This would allow a familiar Advent hymn to be used each Sunday and would permit more time to explore one or two Advent images more fully. The stanzas of the hymn could be sung in response to the recitation of the complementary "O" antiphons. Stanza 1 alone would be used on the First Sunday of Advent, 2 and 3 on the Second Sunday, 4 and 5 on the Third Sunday, and 6 and 7 on the Fourth Sunday. An appropriate collect could conclude the rite, particularly if the lighting of the wreath is also the opening act of worship.

First Sunday of Advent

Old Testament Texts

The Old Testament lesson and the psalm inaugurate the Advent season with a powerful symbol of salvation: Zion. Isaiah 2:1-5 provides a utopian vision of Zion as an end-time reality, while the pilgrimage hymn in Psalm 122 encourages us to claim this salvation in our present lives through worship. Taken together these Old Testament texts provide a strong commentary on Advent. They underscore how Advent points us to a future reality that reaches backwards and embraces us in worship, even while we journey toward its consummation.

The Lesson: *Isaiah 2:1-5*

Zion as God's Goal for Creation

Setting. The imagery of a mountain is central to Isaiah 2:1-5. The word *mountain* is specifically mentioned three times (vv. 2-3), and once it is contrasted to hills (v. 2). A quick look at the words that are associated with the mountain—"the mountain of the house of the Lord" (v. 2) and "the mountain of the Lord" (v. 3)—indicate that the imagery is not geographical, but one of worship and world. The "mountain of the house of the Lord" or (Mount) Zion (v. 3) is quite literally the Temple, the place where God lived and was present with the worshiping community. That God dwells on Mount Zion was one of Israel's central confessions (see Psalm 48). And because of the centrality of this confession along with the desire to live all of life in the presence of God, Israel viewed the entire world from the perspective of the Jerusalem Temple. As a result, Mount Zion constituted the center of the world and all life on earth was evaluated and characterized by how close or how far someone was from God's mountain (the Temple). This centrality of Mount Zion for structuring the whole world was frequently stated through imagery of height as indeed it is in Isaiah 2:2 when God's mountain is described as "the highest of the mountains."

If you are having a difficult time imagining this location of Mount Zion as structuring both worship and world, consider a poster that came out several years ago by Steinberg entitled "A New Yorker's View of the World." The Hudson River is pictured as the outer reaches of the globe because of the centrality of New York City for those who live in it. The poster illustrates how important even secular locations can become in structuring a vision of the world. The Temple in Jerusalem played an even stronger role in Israel's perception of the world, for it was not simply a familiar or comfortable place to live; rather it was the place where God lived.

Structure. Isaiah 2:1-5 is primarily a vision of the future. This eschatological focus is signified in v. 2 with the reference to "the days to come." Central to Isaiah's eschatological vision is the prominence of the mountain of the Lord, and this provides a key for structuring the text. The text can be structured into three parts: an end-time vision of a new creation in which the reality of God's rule is unmistakable (vv. 1-2*a*), the universal social implications of this new world (vv. 2*b*-4), and a prophetic call to faithfulness directed to the worshiping community in the present time because of the good news of God's new future world (v. 5).

Significance. Isaiah 2:1-5 presents a powerful Advent message. The message does not begin with ourselves. It begins with God and God's commitment to a new world, which is conveyed through the mountain imagery in vv. 1-2*a*. The prophet presents radical and even violent creation imagery in these verses by the way in which the mountain of God is pictured as reforming the very topography of the world in its emergence as the highest of all mountains. The word in the NRSV text used to describe this radical change in landscape is that God's mountain is *established* (v. 2*a*), but that word also takes on connotations of *endurance* in the original Hebrew word *nākôn.* Thus the prophet is not simply giving us a snapshot of the end-time but also is telling us that the snapshot is reliable; this picture of the end will endure.

In the next section the prophet fills out the details of the picture by telling us how all people will live in this new world (vv. 2b-4). Here we learn that the mountain of the Lord is like a lighthouse whose beacon extends to the outer reaches of this transformed creation, with the result that no proclamation of God's centrality is required. Instead, all people will spontaneously flock to Zion. We learn their motivation through quotation in v. 3a. The nations encourage one another to go up to the mountain of the Lord to be taught by God and to live in God. The prophet then breaks back in and provides commentary in vv. 3b-4, telling us what the attitude of the nations will be in God's new world. War and the fear of it—which require perpetual preparation—will be useless forms of energy, and as a consequence human activity will be redirected: swords will be refashioned as plowshares and spears as pruning hooks.

Lest we lose ourselves in a dream state about the end-time, the prophet finally turns his attention to us in v. 5. In so doing, the prophet leaves the utopian eschatological world and enters our present one. But even then he does not abandon the eschatological vision. Instead, he pulls it into our world and encourages us, as the people of God in this present time, to "walk in the light of the Lord."

Isaiah 2:1-5 is a text about Advent. It presents a reliable snapshot of the end-time through the imagery of Mount Zion. One day God will recreate this world, and then all will live only by the light of God. Yet Advent is not simply about the future, for aspects of this new world are already taking shape in our own. We celebrate a past incarnation that provides the light for our present worship. Thus we must already walk in the light even as we move toward the light.

The Response: *Psalm 122*

Walking in the Light of Zion

Setting. Psalm 122 picks up where Isaiah 5:1-5 ended. It is not about eschatology, but present-day worship. Psalm 122 is titled "A Song of Ascents of David." The language of ascent in the psalms is most likely language of pilgrimage. The imagery of ascending or going up is a description of the worshiper journeying to the Jerusalem Temple. Thus for the worshiper Psalm 122 is literally about walking in the light of Yahweh in the present time.

Structure. Psalm 122 separates into three parts. The first section is the call to journey to the Temple of the Lord in v. 1. A number of the commentators would extend this section through v. 2; however, this verse fits better as an introduction to the second section of the psalm (vv. 2-5), where the worshiper both gives praise and reflects on the experience of having worshiped in Jerusalem. The psalm closes with a call for prayer in vv. 6-9.

Significance. Our earlier discussion of the role of the Temple for structuring worship and the world is important for interpreting Psalm 122. This is a psalm that thanks God for the very architecture of Jerusalem and the Temple. Yet we would misinterpret the psalm if we limited our interpretation to architecture (just as we would misinterpret the imagery of the mountain if we limited it to geography), for the psalmist is using the architectural imagery in vv. 2-5 to celebrate the salvation of God in the present time through worship. Note in v. 2 how Jerusalem and the Temple are not far off, but realities in which the psalmist is presently standing ("Our feet are standing within your gates, O Jerusalem"). And while basking in this divine presence of worship, the psalmist celebrates the unity of the people of God in v. 3 (the towers of Jerusalem are one) and the instruction that provides direction for life in vv. 4b-5 (the divine decrees and judgments). Yet the psalm does not end here. Verses 6-9 indicate how in this present world the psalmist cannot live all of life in Jerusalem, and in preparing to leave, the psalmist calls for prayer: (1) for the endurance and reliability of God's presence and the worshiping community (vv. 6-7), (2) and for the strength to live an ethical life in harmony with God's decrees and judgments even outside of Jerusalem (vv. 8-9).

The central theme for preaching the Old Testament lessons can be stated in the following manner: Advent is about the reliability of God in bringing about a future world and about how glimmers of this world have already broken into our lives through worship. The Old Testament lessons have provided insight into this reality. They invite us to embrace Isaiah's vision and then, like the psalmist, to pray for the courage to "walk in the light of the Lord" even though in this present time we cannot live our entire lives within Zion.

New Testament Texts

The New Testament epistle and Gospel readings are ripe with Advent themes. Paul's Letter to the Romans declares the nearness of our salvation which is already achieved in Jesus Christ and reminds us that although our salvation is not yet fully realized, the Lordship of Jesus Christ compels us to new patterns of living. Similarly Matthew's Gospel reminds us that we do not know the time of God's promised judgment. If we did, we certainly would be on guard and ready. Since we do not know the time of the day of the Lord, we have but one option—to be always watching, always ready.

The Epistle: *Romans 13:11-14*

God's Time and Our Living

Setting. Although Paul had never visited the believers in Rome, he knew many of them from his travels around the Mediterranean (Paul greets twenty-six persons by name and refers to many others). From these fellow-Christians, Paul seems to know something about the situation in Rome. In chapter 12, the apostle begins to write to the Romans about the practical dimensions of common Christian life—about life in and as the Church—and about life in relation to society, both of which are a life of "love." This pointed, practical material continues to 13:11, where Paul defines the eschatological basis for Christian morality. Paul could have easily moved from 13:10 to 14:1, but the material in 13:11-14 breaks an otherwise natural flow to declare that Christian morality is not merely "being good," rather it is a Christ-created, Christ-empowered life-style.

Structure. This passage comprises two broad movements with smaller directions. Verses 11-12*a* proclaim the eschatological nature of the time, declaring that salvation is drawing ever nearer. Paul speaks in terms of passing time, an anticipated hour, the passing of night, and the arrival of the day. The very mention of "the day" in the eschatologically charged atmosphere of early Christianity would have set minds thinking about the promised final divine judgment on "the day of the Lord." Verses 12*b*-14 follow with a series of negative and positive admonitions. Christians are to move away from evil and toward God's good. Verse 13 defines conduct becoming of "the day" in three negative directives; then, verse 14 instructs the believers to "put on the Lord Jesus Christ" and to avoid gratifying the desires of the flesh.

The material provides a structure that is suggestive for preaching:

1. Declaration of the time
2. Call from "darkness to light"
3. Directions about leaving darkness
4. The Christocentric nature of Christian life that makes no room for sub-Christian behavior

Significance. Christians have the assurance that they are living in a world created and redeemed by God's work in Jesus Christ. Christians live not merely marking or passing time, but looking ahead to what they know God will do, because they already know what God has done in making Jesus Christ Lord. God's future determines the character of current Christian living. It is God's time that calls Christians out of darkness and into light. It is God's work through Christ as Lord that is ending the darkness and bringing the light.

This text informs us that we do not live in a Christlike manner in order that God may better the world through us. Instead, it is because Jesus Christ is Lord, it is because he encompasses us in our everyday existence, that we are freed and empowered to be done with ignoble practices and to live in the light of the day of the Lord (God's standards). Our Christian existence is a consequence, not a cause, of God's redemption of the world.

As is usually the case, this passage consistently employs the plural form of "you" in Greek. The text is addressed to a community of faith, and the admonitions are much more than private commands to decency. Paul wrote to the assembly of the saints in Rome, and while his statements had personal value for each and every believer, none of the apostle's remarks were made to private individuals. Ultimately,

Christian living is God-ordained, Christ-formed, and congregation-ally-centered. While the corporate nature of these remarks is not the primary point of the text, it is necessary that those preaching and forming the liturgy labor to avoid turning the text into a private moral lesson along the lines of Aesop's fables.

The Gospel: *Matthew 24:36-44*

Waiting and Watching for Jesus

Setting. Jesus spoke in a kaleidoscope of images about the future, especially about the day of final judgment. Often he drew on Old Testament images familiar to him, his hearers, and to us, speaking about both Old Testament persons and events. In this passage, the mention of Noah's time before the flood points to the perils of indifference to God. The promise of the coming of the Son of Man and the separation of humans reminds us that God has standards and that ultimately God will and does judge human actions, attitudes, and involvements. Above all, Jesus' teachings make clear that judgment is God's work, and the promised reality of God's future grand assize requires humans to be constantly concerned with and inclined toward God's values.

Structure. In this Gospel lesson, Matthew conflates two pericopes of "Q" material with portions of the little apocalypse of Mark 13. Mark 13:32 parallels Matthew 24:36 and Mark 13:35 parallels Matthew 24:42. Mark 13:33-34 is omitted by Matthew at this point in his Gospel, but he has similar, though more elaborate, material at 25:13-15 (possibly derived from a "Q" tradition, since there is a parallel in Luke 19:12-13 that is also quite different from Mark in its development, but similar to Matthew 25:13-15 to a degree). There is strong similarity between Matthew 24:37-41 and Luke 17:26-35 and between Matthew 24:43-44 and Luke 12:39-40. Thus, for study, the comparisons are

Matt. 24:36	par	Mark 13:32;
Matt. 24:37-41	par	Luke 17:26-35;
Matt. 24:42	par	Mark 13:35;
Matt. 24:43-44	par	Luke 12:39-40.

The material is remarkably complex. It brings together noticeably disparate traditions and testifies to the rich practice of reflection on the life and teaching of Jesus in the earliest Church. The eschatological outlook of this passage was not merely common but foundational in the life of early Christianity as is evident from the many similar texts in places like Luke 12 and 17; Acts 3; I Corinthians 15; Colossians 3; I Thessalonians 4; II Thessalonians 2; I Peter 14; and Revelation 22.

Significance. Verse 36 is the first part of a bracket around the larger section, 24:36-44, finding its complement in 24:44. The verse addresses the theme of the day of final judgment—it articulates indirectly a positive expectation of the coming of that day, and it declares directly that no one but God alone knows when the day of judgment will come.

In vv. 37-41 the story of Noah (from Genesis 5:28–9:29—see especially Genesis 6) becomes a prototype of the world situation faced by the Christians, but notice that in Matthew's reference to "the days of Noah" the focus is not on wickedness as it is in the Genesis account, but on the lack of concern with impending judgment. The problem addressed in Matthew is not immorality but lethargy, self-absorption, and indifference to God's immanent presence in judgment.

Still further Old Testament material lies behind the mention of the Son of Man. Both the title, "the Son of Man," and the idea of his coming draw on not only the imagery of passages like Daniel 7 in the Old Testament, but also on the teaching of the non-canonical book of I Enoch, which itself was a vital source of inspiration for both the ministry of Jesus and the life of the early Church.

The imagery of sudden separation of men in the field and women at the mill shows that God has standards that, when applied in judgment, make crucial distinctions between persons. In this prejudgment world, human actions count for something and will be assessed by God. From the statements in this text, however, we cannot distinguish one person from another, precisely because final judgment is totally God's affair. Something other than the actions named—work in the fields and the mills—is the basis of God's judgment. From the context, it can only be whether or not the persons are watching, that is, how they are living their lives in relation to God. Are they concerned with God or with themselves? Are they "watching"? Furthermore, there is an emphasis in the imagery of this text on suddenness. Not only is God's judgment unexpected; it is quick and decisive. Here, there is no debate or appeal when God acts in judgment.

Verse 42 sounds a positive directive—not merely despite, but specifically because no one other than God knows the time of the final day of judgment. Therefore, Christians are to watch! Their assurance is that the Lord is coming, but this is not information that establishes a relaxed or privileged life-style; rather it necessitates vigilance. The declaration in this verse is not a threat, but a call; not an alarm, but an opportunity; not a cause for dismay, but a reason for hope.

Verses 43-44 reiterate the main themes of this section of Matthew's Gospel. The metaphor of the thief in the night expresses the unexpected nature of the coming of Christ and recognizes the lack of precise knowledge about the time. It was a popular figure for the coming of Christ in early Christianity as is evinced by the use of the same image in I Thess. 5:2. The image is not, however, a socially pleasant one; and it communicates effectively the possible perils of God's judgment and the necessity of an alert and attentive Christian hope for God's final historical advent in Christ.

Advent 1: The Celebration

Today's lessons appropriately inaugurate another year of worship by setting a scene in which worship is the context for waiting for judgment and the establishment of God's reign. The references to Mount Zion in the Old Testament lesson and the psalm lead us to a new consideration of "Glorious Things of Thee Are Spoken" as a hymn for today, and in turn its line "safe we feed upon the manna" reinforces the practice of beginning the liturgical year with Holy Communion. The theme of judgment calls for some form of confession of sin somewhere in the service. Today might also serve as an occasion to overcome the purely patriotic connotations of "The Battle Hymn of the Republic." Its primary images are thoroughly biblical and quite in keeping with the mood of the lessons, while the last stanza, "In the beauty of the lilies," relates the day to the coming celebration of Christmas. The epistle lesson is the source for the traditional Advent collect, "Almighty God, give us grace to cast away the works of darkness."

The preacher's commitment to the calendar and the lectionary as primary vehicles for conveying the Word of God to the community of faith will be tested at the outset in many congregations. To the degree that preachers are members of the community, sharing its civil and cultural biases and allegiances, they may feel a bit foolish preaching about "reveling and drunkenness" (epistle) to persons already anticipating December's office parties. It is easy to feel merely a killjoy in the midst of a consumer society that values immediate gratification above all else and that, by this First Sunday of Advent, has already embarked upon an orgy of sentimental materialism. When the television commercials from the local police are warning us to lock our gifts in the trunk and to take special precautions when we are away from home during the holiday season, the Church begins the year with Jesus announcing that he is a thief! The preacher might wish, on the basis of the Gospel evidence, to examine what it is that Jesus might steal if he breaks into our lives.

Because of the epistle, the preacher might wish to remind the congregation of an earlier member of the community, St. Augustine, who relates his own conversion to this very passage:

> I was . . . weeping in the most bitter contrition of my heart, when, lo, I heard the voice as of a boy or girl, I know not which, coming from a neighboring house, chanting, and oft repeating, "Take up and read; take up and read." . . . I grasped, opened, and in silence read that paragraph on which my eyes first fell, "Not in rioting and drunkenness, not in chambering and wantonness, not in strife and envying; but put ye on the Lord Jesus Christ, and make not provision for the flesh, to fulfil the lusts thereof." No further would I read, nor did I need; for instantly, as the sentence ended—by a light, as it were, of security infused into my heart—all the gloom of doubt vanished away. [*Confessions*, Book 8 in J. G. Pilkington, trans., Philip Schaff, ed., *A Select Library of the Nicene and Post-Nicene Fathers of the Christian Church,* vol. 1 (Grand Rapids: Eerdmans, 1983), pp. 127-28]

Second Sunday of Advent

Old Testament Texts

The future looms large during Advent. We are, after all, entering into a sacred time of hope when we look with expectation toward the consummation of our salvation. If, however, we become too preoccupied with our future, we may miss the salvific work of God in our present lives, which actually grounds our Advent faith. Our Old Testament texts for this Second Sunday of Advent confront us with this danger. Both are messianic texts that soar to breathtaking heights in envisioning the future that God has in store for us. Yet upon closer reading, one begins to wonder whether Isaiah 11:1-10 and Psalm 72:1-7, 18-19 are not actually more concerned with God's present salvation than with a utopian future.

The Lesson: *Isaiah 11:1-10*

Celebrating the Messianic Rule

Setting. Isaiah 11:1-10 reflects Israel's royal theology. Second Samuel 7 provides some background to understanding this theological perspective. This narrative is about David's desire to build God a house. In the course of the story we learn that God is not particularly interested in having a house, and in the light of this, the narrative undergoes a reversal when God promises instead to build David a "house." The reversal of course is not about a building but about the promise of a dynasty. Although the promise is presently couched in certain conditions (v. 14), these conditions are not able to alter what is clearly an unconditional promise (vv. 9-13, 16)—namely, that David's house will rule forever. This promise is both sociopolitical and theological. Theologically, it means that one from David's line will always be God's "anointed one" (the Hebrew word *messiah* *[māšîăḥ])* not because every king will necessarily be faithful, but because God will be faithful to this promise. Thus Israel's royal theology is rooted in grace or election. The content of the grace is that the king, as God's messiah, will have a special relationship with God that is qualitatively different from the people at large. Psalm 72:1 reflects this belief when the king is called God's "royal son." The political and social effect of this theology is that when the king is fulfilling this special relationship as God's messiah, divine blessing and well-being are mediated to the social order.

Structure. Isaiah 11:1-10 is the combination of at least two distinct texts. Isaiah 11:1-9 describes the role of the messianic king within the Israelite community of faith. This text is not necessarily eschatological, for it lacks a clear eschatological introduction, such as "in that day." Isaiah 11:10, on the other hand, describes the role of the messianic king among the nations with clear eschatological language, for note how it begins with "in that day." When the two texts are combined they separate into three parts: first, vv. 1-5 describe the qualities of the Davidic king (vv. 1-3*a*) along with the king's social obligations (vv. 3*b*-5); second, vv. 6-9 describe how nature itself could be remade if the king consistently and faithfully fulfills the messianic role, and hence these verses move implicitly into the future in picturing a paradise where all forms of life live together in peace; and third, v. 10 moves explicitly into the future by outlining the universal social implications of the messianic king.

Significance. Isaiah 11:1-10 is a breathtaking text about salvation. What makes this text so breathtaking is that it is not a prophetic daydream that we the readers are allowed to place wishfully into the future. The absence of clear eschatological indicators in the opening verses underscores this point. Note how the spirit-filled characteristics of the messianic king in vv. 1-3*a* are intimately linked with the present life of the people of God in vv. 3*b*-5. This is in keeping with Israel's royal theology. The election of the king was not simply a theological idea that legitimized political power while promising a brighter future one day. Rather, the special messianic role of the king had to be seen in the everyday life of the people through the transforming qualities of righteousness and justice (v. 5). Although the text ends by moving toward the future with a utopian description of a new creation (vv. 6-9) and a universal vision of messianic rule (v. 10), we would misinterpret this text if we made these two sections the point of emphasis, without seeing that it is the messianic qualities of righteousness and justice made visible in the community of faith that allows the text to move to its grand conclusion.

Such a strong messianic text in Advent certainly invites a christological interpretation. Jesus is indeed the branch from Jesse. A christological interpretation of Isaiah 11:1-10 should emphasize even more the present character of this text, for we are now nearly two thousand years into the messianic reign of Jesus. Our focus, therefore, in reading this text should not be exclusively on Jesus and his Spirit-filled messianic role, for it has long since been reliably fulfilled. Our emphasis should be on whether the social implications of his rule are evident in the community of faith. Do we see his righteousness and justice in our communities of faith?

The Response: *Psalm 72:1-7, 18-19*

Praying for the Messianic Rule

Setting. Psalm 72 is a prayer for the Davidic monarch. It is probably called a Psalm of Solomon because of reference to the one who built the house of God. This royal psalm was most likely part of a larger liturgy that celebrated the enthronement of the king. Although the original setting of the psalm is difficult to confirm, what is clear is that this prayer for the king is not about the distant future, but about Israel's present life. The emphasis in Psalm 72:1-7, 18-19—on righteousness and justice as qualities that must be mediated through the messianic king into the present life of the community of faith—provides a close parallel to Isaiah 11:1-10.

Structure. Psalm 72:1-7, 18-19 divides into two sections, which parallel the structure of Isaiah 11:1-10. Verses 1-7 are a prayer of intercession for the king to rule the people of Israel with righteousness and justice. As in Isaiah 10:1-9, the focus on these verses is not

31

eschatological, but a petition for ethical behavior by the king in the present time. Verses 18-19 enlarge the scope of the king's rule and provides a more eschatological interpretation of the messianic king. This larger vision of the messiah parallels the function of Isaiah 11:10 where the rule of the Davidic king was also shot off into the distant future and placed in the larger context of the world.

Significance. A closer look at the structure of Psalm 72:1-7, 18-19 underscores several important points about God's salvation in our present lives, which could be used in preaching. First, v. 1 underscores how the ethics of the king are not simply humanitarian ideals, but qualities that must be learned from God. It is God's justice and righteousness that are being requested. Second, vv. 2-4 underscore how the divine attributes must go beyond the character of the king and become evident in the social transformation of Israel. We learn that the oppressor must be crushed and that the cause of the needy must be defended. Third, vv. 5-7 underscore the community's dependence on God with the petition that God's social transformation of Israel through the messianic king endure throughout time. Finally, vv. 18-19, through proclamation to the glory of God, move the focus of the prayer beyond the boundaries of Israel.

Psalm 72:1-7, 18-19 emphasizes even more strongly than Isaiah 11:1-10 how important it is for us to claim God's salvation in our present lives as a ground for our Advent faith. Certainly we do not want to interpret Psalm 72:1-7, 18-19 as a prayer for Jesus. Verse 1 presupposes that the king does not have the justice and righteousness of God, hence the petition for God to train him. As post-Easter Christians we are not in doubt about whether Jesus embodies the justice and righteousness of God. Thus we are also not in doubt about whether Jesus, as our messiah, is able to mediate divine blessing and well-being to the social order. Consequently as a prayer for the messianic king, Psalm 72:1-7, 18-19 loses much of its force for Christians. But it acquires urgency as a prayer for the messianic community in the present time. Given the reliability of our messiah, do we embody the divine qualities of righteousness and justice within the community of faith? And do we mediate divine blessing and well-being to the larger social order?

New Testament Texts

The reading from Romans emphasizes hope in relation to the coming of the promised "root of Jesse," an heir in the line of David. Paul frames this hope in terms of the salvation and the joy of the Gentiles over whom the promised one will reign. The text from Matthew offers a series of cameos related to John the Baptist: his preaching, his person, the popular response to his work, his confrontation with the Pharisees and Sadducees, and most important, his prediction of the greater one who was coming after him.

The Epistle: *Romans 15:4-13*

God's Work and Our Hope

Setting. Paul wrote to the Romans as he was about to go to Jerusalem to deliver the collection he and his co-workers had assembled for assisting the impoverished among the believers in Jerusalem. Yet, in writing, the apostle looked beyond delivering the collection in anticipation of the next major phase of his apostleship, a mission to Spain. He wrote to win a reception for himself and the gospel he preached in Rome, because in order for a Spanish mission to be successful Paul would need a base in the West (Rome), as he had had such a center of operations in the East (Antioch). After a lengthy discussion of the gospel (chap. 1–8) and its ultimate meaning for all humanity—Jews and Gentiles alike—(chap. 9–11), Paul addresses the believers in Rome about their specific situation (chap. 12–15). Chapter 14 begins to discuss differing opinions about what composes a Christian life-style, and this reflection continues through v. 6. At v. 7 Paul recasts his advice, although perhaps continuing along the same lines, in terms of the relationship of Jewish-Christians and Gentile-Christians. He then addresses the Romans about his future plans to visit them on his way to work in Spain.

Structure. The passage falls into two distinct parts: vv. 4-6 concludes the discussion of the difference of opinion about Christian life-style. There is a linear logic in vv. 4-6: (1) instruction in the scriptures yields (2) hope in which (3) God unifies the believers (4) who mutually glorify God. This thought pattern makes a sensible sermon outline.

Verses 7-13 admonish diverse believers (Jewish and Gentile, or, to cast the matter in functional rather than ethnic terms, law-observant and non-law-observant Christians) toward mutuality, taking Christ's own acceptance of humanity as the model of Christian behavior (v. 7). Having made this point, Paul offers a kind of historical sketch of the reality of Christ's saving work—he came in service to the circumcised (the Jews or the law-observant) as a fulfillment of the promises to the patriarchs in order that he might ultimately extend mercy to the Gentile (the non-law-observant; vv. 8-9). Paul then engages in an elaborate scripture-based meditation on the marvelous character of God's work in Christ, which ultimately fills Jews and Gentiles— law-observant and non-law-observant—with joyous, peaceful, and faithful hope.

Significance. Having advised the Romans to forego claims to personal rights or privileges for the sake of others (vv. 1-2) and having quoted Psalm 69:6 as a proof-from-prophecy (v. 3), Paul declares that scripture serves to instruct Christians in such a manner that hope is instilled in believers (v. 4). He then utters a wish that God may unify the Roman Christians (Jewish and Gentile) into a Christlike whole, which will eventuate in its harmony in the glorification of God (v. 5). One may focus on the crucial role of scripture in providing instruction that sets up expectations which are in turn confirmed in God's work in Jesus Christ. Knowing God's ways and that God is incontrovertibly faithful establishes hope in the lives of believers. Indeed, focusing on God and God's faithfulness takes the attention of Christians away from themselves and their differences and provides a common basis of hope in the one God of all believers. There is a stark lesson in this text: Christian unity is not established in common human points of view; rather, hope in the one God who came—first to the Jews and then to the Gentiles, but ultimately for both together—cuts across dividing lines (even of sacred doctrine) to the only one who can unify a fragmented humanity (vv. 7-13). God's work in Christ to create harmony is the source of our hope, and our hope is the motivation for our joy and peace in believing, which leads us to praise God together with one voice (v. 6).

The Gospel: *Matthew 3:1-12*

God's Straight Path: Comfort of the Afflicted and Affliction of the Comfortable

Setting. Chapters 1 and 2 of Matthew tell the story of the birth and early childhood years of Jesus. With chapter 3 we move ahead some thirty years, and we refocus our attention on the ministry of John the Baptist. The Baptist appears after an interval of two hundred years in which Israel had known no prophets. Thus John is a transitional figure in Matthew's Gospel. Having told of Jesus' early years in Bethlehem, Egypt, and Nazareth, Matthew quickly recounts the appearance and work of the Baptist (3:1-12); and then, he tells of the coming of the full-grown Jesus from Galilee to the Jordan in Judea, where—through baptism at the hand of John—Jesus moves into his own ministry.

Structure. These twelve verses report a remarkable amount of information about John. Verses 1-3 report John's appearance in the wilderness and give a sketch of the content of his preaching. Verse 4 describes John's dress and diet—both of which are reminiscent of the prophets of the Old Testament. Verses 5-6 tell how the masses went out to John and responded positively to his proclamation, but vv. 7-10 tell how John upbraided the Pharisees and Sadducees (who, remarkably, were coming to him for baptism!) with a message about the eschatological nature of the time. Finally, vv. 11-12 report John's prediction of the greater one who was coming after him, an eschatological figure set to separate humanity in powerful judgment.

Significance. Although the text coheres around the character John the Baptist, meditation on his person per se, even as a paragon of radical faith, does not fit the mood or focus of the Advent season. Rather, those working at preaching and liturgy should move directly to the Baptist's message, which issues a call for repentance and, in turn, directs those who believe and repent to make straight God's path. The basis for this call to change and devotion to God's ways is clear as John declares the nearness of God's power. The movement of God toward humanity calls forth the needed change of direction on the part of human beings and motivates the subsequent efforts of repentant humans in God's behalf. The logic is plain: God moves toward us in our sinful condition. God requires and enables us to change the direction of our lives, so that we go God's ways and not our own.

The response to John's proclamation is noteworthy. Numbers of people hear the good news of God's approach, and they are moved to change their ways. Yet, all those coming are not received equally. Some are baptized, but John confronts others—here the Pharisees and the Sadducees, who come for baptism, but who are actually quite secure in their assumed relationship to God. John blasts the self-satisfied and exposes the inadequacy of their motives in seeking baptism. Why they come is not clear from the text, but John's remarks expose their deficiencies. The repudiation of these folks is not absolute, however, for John continues to demand that they "bear fruit" as he warns them of impending judgment and destruction. The division among the people in the ministry of John is a foreshadowing of the grand assize that John anticipates and proclaims. In other words, John preaches and ministers in such a way that the promised future is already present in his own activity. In Advent we are called forth in hope to God's future, but we must always remember that God's future is now at work making claims on our lives, setting us moving in new directions, forming our present patterns of living.

John's proclamation took on concrete character with the announcement of the "greater one" who was coming after the Baptist. John's prophecy (in person, word, and deed he recalls the prophets of Israel) unites the past, the present, and the future. God's word in the past has meaning in the present, because God moves from the future into our present! The dynamics of this vision of God are crucial. Without the future, a memory of the past has little more power to effect the present than a romantic, nostalgic remembrance, but without the past, claims about the future in relation to the present are little more than wishful thinking. In turn, reflection on the past and the future, idealized with no real meaning for life in the present, is at best an academic exercise.

In the Advent season, when Christians are inevitably anticipating the celebration of the birth of Jesus, it may prove beneficial to contrast the rather frightening figure foretold by the Baptist with the typical gentle Jesus, meek and mild, of popular piety. The Christ Child who was sent from God was a compassionate divine bequest to humanity. But it is well to remember that the sweet baby Jesus is the one who died a brutal death on Calvary's tree.

Advent 2: The Celebration

On the First Sunday of Advent our concentration was on the Church's eschatological hope, the consummation of all things under the rule of Christ. We were as "far out" in time as it is possible to get. All of the lessons today remind Christians that "spiritually we are all Semites." The Old Testament lesson beautifully expresses the ideal of messianic rule; the psalm has been expressed in christological terms in the hymn "Hail to the Lord's Anointed."

The scriptures being referred to in the epistle are the scriptures of Judaism, and John the Baptist strides onto the gospel stage straight out of the pages of the Hebrew prophetic tradition. In his preaching, we hear the Old Testament prophets. All of these references to our roots in Judaism invite the use of a modern hymn "The King of Glory Comes," by W. F. Jabusch, set to an Israeli folk tune. It appears as No. 963 in *The United Methodist Supplement to the Book of Hymns* and No. 267 in *Worship II: A Hymnal for Roman Catholic Parishes* (GIA Publications), and it can be effectively used as a responsive choral call to worship.

Following the suggestion in the exegesis that today's psalm "acquires urgency as a prayer for the messianic community in the present time," how can it provide an agenda for the day's intercessions and petitions?

Major themes involve repentance, hope, and the scriptures. The Old Testament lesson provides a description of the community we are called to be; our failures at this point might be the focus of the prayer of confession for the day. The scriptural emphasis was discussed in the opening essay on Advent. A traditional symbol for hope is the anchor and would be an appropriate visual for today, particularly if the sermon picked up that theme.

The preceding commentaries on today's lessons have made clear that the preacher has a great variety of texts and topics from which to choose. Through them all, however, there remains the issue of the relationship between Judaism and Christianity, and what it means for Christians to apply Isaiah's messianic vision to themselves. John the Baptist, to whom the Christian tradition has given the title of saint, represents the prophetic tradition of the Hebrew Scriptures. His preaching of repentance is addressed to the Pharisees and Sadducees, possibly making it easy for Christian hearers to shrug it off, as I have known some to do, saying, "That was addressed to the Jews, not to us." Christian anti-Semitism is frequently justified on the basis of such passages as this, and Christian preachers need to recognize their complicity in prejudice if they never address the problem. The preacher's task today is to help the hearers identify themselves as the contemporary Pharisees and Sadducees, respectable folk, wanting to do the right thing, proud of their Christian heritage. Expectation and repentance are inextricably linked in the Gospel. What has the "fruit worthy of repentance" to do with the vision of the messianic community that is described in Isaiah? To do with the Church that is still expectant? To do with the Church and Israel waiting together? To do with the Church and Israel called to be a light to the nations, to serve the One who is to "defend the cause of the poor . . . , give deliverance to the needy, and crush the oppressor"? Does the emergence of a rapidly growing, vital Christianity in the Third World, particularly Africa, serve in any way as a commentary to Western churches on Matthew 3:9? In all of the preparations for Christmas, are the fruits of repentance being harvested?

Third Sunday of Advent

Old Testament Texts

Our Old Testament lessons for the third week of Advent explore hope. Isaiah 35 proclaims the inevitability of God's salvation, even when we find ourselves at a great distance from Zion in situations that appear to be hopeless. Psalm 146:5-10 is a hymn of praise that calls us to trust in God because of God's enduring reliability.

The Lesson: *Isaiah 35:1-10*

Hope for the Hopeless

Setting. Theophanies are biblical texts that describe the appearance of God. The oldest theophany traditions in Israel follow a format in which the forces of nature would respond to the approach of God (see Judges 5:4-5). Although Isaiah 35:1-10 is a relatively late text—often assigned to second Isaiah or third Isaiah—note how it still follows this pattern of providing a response of nature to the appearance of "the glory of the Lord" (vv. 1-2), which is present for the purpose of bringing about a new salvation. The theophany of God in Isaiah 35:1-10 must be read in the larger context of Isaiah 34, which also describes the presence of God, but for the purpose of judgment rather than salvation. Isaiah 34:2-4 describes how God will slaughter the nations, how the stench of their corpses will rise, how the hosts of heaven will rot away and the skies roll up like a scroll. The juxtaposition of Isaiah 34 and 35 underscores the two-sided character of theophany. It can simultaneously be experienced as judgment (Isaiah 34) and salvation (Isaiah 35), as devastation (Isaiah 34) and re-creation (Isaiah 35). Hope and trust are the dividing lines between Isaiah 34–35. Hope in human power is the undoing of the nations, in contrast to the remnant who trust in God.

Structure. What do the remnant hope for? Isaiah 35:1-10 divides into a description of the reappearance of God (vv. 1-6*a*) and a new salvation (vv. 6*b*-10). The reappearance of God includes a reaction of both nature (vv. 1-2) and God's remnant (vv. 3-6*a*). The new salvation that accompanies God's reappearance includes a remaking of the desert wasteland into a fertile oasis (vv. 6*b*-7), the construction of a holy highway for a new exodus through the desert (vv. 8-9), and the return of God's remnant to Zion (v. 10).

Significance. When Isaiah 35:1-10 is read against the background of Isaiah 34, the radical reversal of salvation is underscored both for humanity and for creation itself. As the nations are destroyed and their culture turned into a wasteland for jackals and other wild beasts (Isaiah 34:8-12), Isaiah 35 describes how God can simultaneously re-create new life for the people of God. Wilderness can be turned into lush farmland (vv. 1-2, 6*b*-7) and a salvation road can be fashioned where one had not been thought possible (vv. 8-9). In addition, humans too can be remade (vv. 5-6*a*) to walk the salvation road light-footed and singing all the way to Zion itself.

The central theme in preaching Isaiah 35 is that hope is alive even at times of apparent hopelessness. The radical reversals of nature and humanity that are presented to the reader as inevitable events that must accompany the appearance of God provide both motivation and the firm basis for hope in God that is central to Advent. These radical reversals underscore how our present experience cannot be the final word on the character or reliability of God's salvation. One of our tasks in this Advent season is to look at ourselves and at our larger community of faith through the eyes of the prophet Isaiah and take on his words of encouragement from vv. 3-4. We must ask ourselves whose "weak hands" must "be strengthened," or whose "feeble knees" must be "made firm" again. Where is fear taking over and hope fading? Who especially needs the message of Advent this season that God will inevitably "come and save" us?

The Response: *Psalm 146:5-10*

Celebrating Our Hope

Setting. Psalm 146 is a hymn of praise. The lectionary begins at v. 5 where the motif of hope in God is introduced. Even though the lectionary reading appears to have been made in order to accentuate the theme of hope, the preacher might use all of Psalm 146 for two reasons. First, the quality of praise is lost without the strong opening in vv. 1-2. And second, hope in God in vv. 5-10 is being contrasted to hope in human power in vv. 3-4. The contrast is important, for it underscores how trust or hope is essential to our very character, and hence how we must place our trust in some power either human or divine. Thus, when read in its entirety, Psalm 146 picks up a theme that was discussed earlier in the contrast between Isaiah 34 and 35—namely, that where we place our hope can be our undoing or our remaking. Psalm 146 is a celebration of how hope in God is our remaking.

Structure. The commentaries separate Psalm 146 in a number of different ways. There is agreement that vv. 1-2 provide an introduction of praise, the contrast between trust in humans (vv. 3-4) and trust in God (vv. 5-7 or vv. 5-9) is divided into at least two distinct sections, with the affirmation of Zion providing a conclusion in v. 10. Although such outlines are very workable, the psalm would more simply be divided between the introductory praise in vv. 1-2 and a larger section of vv. 3-10 entitled, "alternatives for human trust."

Significance. Psalm 146 provides both a meditation on and a celebration of hope. As we noted above, the double-sided nature of hope is explored through the contrast between vv. 3-4 and vv. 5-10. Verses 3-4 describe the disastrous results of anchoring our hope in human power. Through a pun on the word *human* (Hebrew, *'ādām*; English, *Adam*) and *earth* (Hebrew, *'ādāmāh*; English, *earth* or *ground*) the psalmist warns us against trusting in human power. The text reads:

> Do not put your trust in princes,
> in mortals [*'ādām*], in whom there is no help [literally, salvation].
> When their breath departs, they return to the earth [*'ādāmāh*];
> on that very day their plans perish.

41

The structure of the text provides the logic of the psalmist's argument, which includes a statement about salvation and creation. Human power cannot help or save us, because in the end it lacks the power to re-create, with the result that *'ādām* (human) is simply absorbed back into *'ādāmāh* (earth). Without the power to re-create there is no possibility for the radical reversal of creation and humanity envisioned in Isaiah 35:1-10.

In vv. 5-10 the psalmist presents the contrast. Verse 5 provides the topic sentence for this section: hope instead in the help of the God of Jacob. Verses 6-10 provide the psalmist's argument, which again includes statements about salvation and creation. Verses 5-7*a* describe the character of God as both creator (maker of heaven, earth, sea, and everything in them) and savior (one who keeps faith, executes justice, and provides food to the hungry). Verses 7*b*-10 describe the activity of God. As savior, God will bring about a series of radical reversals that are filled with hope for the people of God (from setting the prisoners free to bringing the wicked to ruin), and as the creator, God will not be absorbed back into the earth but reign forever. Thus for the psalmist hope in God is reliable because, as both creator and savior, God's salvific plans do not perish, like human plans.

New Testament Texts

One is easily tempted to turn the words of James into a moral lesson, which is a mistake, as will be seen by examining the text carefully. In turn, the reading from the Gospel is a complex collection of distinguishable traditions that may be used in concert or individually for worship and preaching, because the themes operate in a complementary fashion but are worthy of individual consideration.

The Epistle: *James 5:7-10*

Patience in Anticipation

Setting. James offers much practical advice on religion. Insodoing the book stands in a long line of similar Jewish literature concerned with wisdom and ethics. James assumes there are two contrasting spheres of existence, one dominated by God and the other manipulated by the devil. James gives advice for appropriate living in God's realm, and he steadily warns against the devil and the ways of the world.

The move in James 5:7 to advocate "patience" among the believers seems to be an odd turn from the immediately preceding material that warned against friendship with the world and denounced the wealthy citizens of this world. But, at 5:7, James shifts his point of view from the world to the believers. Hearing about the scandalous ways of the rich could easily arouse the indignity of less affluent believers, so James wards off any problem his remarks may have provoked. The call to "patience"—literally to having a "long-temper"—is a call to a godly life. Throughout the Septuagint and in other portions of the New Testament, God is said to "be long-tempered" or to have "a long-temper." And here James explores some essential dimensions of Christian patience.

Structure. The text is a series of four remarks that are loosely connected through concerns with patience and the coming of the Lord. The logic and sequence of the text are suggestive for proclamation and worship. First, James makes a positive admonition to patience, which he explains using the metaphor of a farmer waiting on crops. Second, James repeats the charge to patience, but now he bases the disposition of patience clearly on the promise of the coming of the Lord. Third, James advises against Christians grumbling against one another. As with the positive advice to "be patient," this negative counsel, "do not grumble against one another," is related to the future, but in this instance to the promise of judgment, which was an inherent part of early Christian belief that the Lord's coming was immanent. Fourth, James refers to the prophets as patterns of the "suffering and patience" to which he has called his congregation.

Significance. James's call to patience is not a mere moral appeal, as is clear from a consideration of the entire text. The patience that he demands is not only the result of a desire to do good. Rather, it is the result of a firm confidence in the Lord as the one who will make good on his promise to come in judgment. In particular these verses reflect the character of life lived in confident anticipation of the fulfillment of divine promises: First, as v. 8 makes plain, Christians live with an altered point of view. Believers interpret the present in terms of the

Lord's future, which radically alters their life-styles. Christians live as someone reading a mystery novel after having read the last chapter of the book first; knowing the outcome produces an informed reading of the book. Second, v. 9 unpacks the significance of this Christian perspective on life by recognizing the reality of altered relationships. Christians do not grumble against one another, perhaps because of the fear of judgment, but even more so because they have the freedom established through the promise of judgment. If the Lord promises to judge, then believers leave that work to the Lord and do not engage in such activity themselves. Believers suffer rather than grumble because of the transforming hope of the Lord's promised coming in judgment. After a jury brings a guilty verdict, a plaintiff awaits the judge's sentencing of the defendant with a different attitude from that held before the trial began. Third, v. 10 summarizes the meaning of the altered abilities of those who await the Lord; they have patience and the capacity to suffer because of the freedom brought by the hope given in the Lord's promises. A factory worker manages a difficult assignment differently fifteen minutes before quitting time from the way he or she approached the task at the beginning of the day.

In summary, this text from James is far more than a small moral lesson. It is a profound call to experience the freedom of confidence in the Lord. The outcome of the radical trust in God's promises to which James calls believers gives an altered perspective, altered relationships, and altered abilities—all as results of the Lord's empowering promises.

The Gospel: *Matthew 11:2-11*

Recognizing Christ and Recognizing the Time

Setting. The incidents reported in these verses come at the beginning of the third patterned section of narrative plus subsequent discourse in the Gospel. The entire unit occupies 11:2–13:53. As the lead incidents in this segment of Matthew, these verses register crucial themes and perspectives that will come into play throughout the larger unit—namely, wondering about Jesus, the evidence for Jesus, the challenge of Jesus, the changes brought by Jesus.

Structure. Verses 2-6 form a subunit in this text, and they are neatly arranged. First, vv. 2-3 show John wondering and asking about Jesus. Then, vv. 4-5 record the content and aims of Jesus' ministry and function as the evidence for John's reflection upon who Jesus is and how he does (or does not) fulfill established expectations. Finally, v. 6 states a maxim that recognizes the factually divisive character of Jesus' work.

In turn, vv. 7-11 cohere as the next distinguishable section of the lectionary text. Whereas vv. 2-6 operated from the perspective of John's questions about Jesus and Jesus' reply, vv. 7-11 show us Jesus' view of the Baptist. First, in vv. 7-9 Jesus poses a series of questions, rhetorical and didactic. Jesus offers and rejects superficial, nontheological evaluations of John; and then he registers the theological assessment of John as a prophet, more than a prophet! Next, Jesus makes pronouncements related to John both by quoting scripture to show how John fulfills God's purposes and by directly declaring his own estimation of John's greatness.

Significance. The lectionary focuses on this passage during Advent because of the phrase ''the one who is to come''; but one should notice that while the text has an element of future expectation, it also makes strong statements about the realization of hopes and expectations in the historical ministry of Jesus. In a penetrating fashion, these verses identify the real presence of the future hope of God's faithful servants in the person and work of Jesus Christ. During Advent there is a strong tendency toward worship and proclamation that frame faith in terms of the future, hope, and expectation, but these verses also remind us that Christian faith is, even in its eschatological dimensions, fully in touch with the realities of historical existence.

Verses 2-6 are deep reflection on Christology. First, John hears about what Jesus is doing in his ministry, but there is no neat fit with standard messianic expectations. In Jesus' time, people tended to expect a messiah who would exterminate wickedness in all its forms. This conviction was interpreted on the one hand to mean that the sinful elements in Judaism would experience a wrathful rejection, and on the other hand that the political forces that restricted the full freedom of Israel would be overthrown as Israel moved into a position of supremacy. But Jesus was no Jewish Caesar, and he did not pour out wrath universally in repudiation of evil. Though John recognized enough of God's power at work to indicate that Jesus might be the long-awaited messiah, still he had reservations about identifying Jesus with the terms of his expectations. Yet, John showed an open-ended attitude of faith. He did not sit in judgment on Jesus, but rather he asked Jesus himself whether he was the coming one. Next, Jesus uses images of salvation from Isaiah to describe the character of his ministry. Jesus ties his ministry of liberating humans from the hindrances that bound them to the expectations articulated in the Old Testament. Thus he makes plain that his work is a fulfillment of Israel's hopes for God's salvation, though he does not claim to fulfill all of Israel's hopes. With these images from scripture used to describe his ministry, Jesus places his case before John. Jesus avoids a mere *yes* or *no* answer, for such a reply would be a sheer proposition to be accepted or rejected. Rather, with the language of faith he portrays his work before the faithful John, who will comprehend Jesus as God grants it. Finally, Jesus issues a pronouncement that sums up the state of evaluations of his ministry. For those who see in Jesus the fulfillment of God's promises, which requires them to redefine their definition of messiah, there is blessing. But there is no blessing for those who insist that Jesus match their own expectations, which allows them to define the messiah rather than allowing the messiah to give them a new point of view.

Verses 7-11 show that a commonsense human analysis of John will not provide real understanding of his person and work. Rather, a theological point of view is required for correct comprehension. The text confronts the form and content of much preaching that is all too intent upon reasoning about God rather than insisting upon a reframing and reevaluating of our experience from God's perspective. The challenge here is to bring the text to life as a present power rather than to talk about it as a mere fact. Fortunately in this text Jesus himself offers us a model for operations: He gives a theological re-reading of John in vv. 10-11. John is understood (as was Jesus) in relation to scripture—he is a prophet, and one of greatness. With the connection made between contemporaneous reality and scripture, Jesus moves beyond the employment of texts to declare that he and his hearers stand in a new, altered time and space. With the advent of the kingdom of God, present in Jesus' person and work, time and space have been recast. The Kingdom with its saving power brings a wholeness (verses 4-5) that is superior to even the best (John the Baptist) that the world-without-the-Kingdom has known.

Advent 3: The Celebration

The First Sunday of Advent catapulted us to the end of time. The Second Sunday rooted us in the tradition of Israel, its prophets and writings. Today the Old and New Testaments meet in the persons of John the Baptist and Jesus. Our time travel is slowing down a bit, and we can now identify ourselves in a present that has both a past and a future.

In the Gospel for today, Jesus affirms the value of the Old Testament tradition out of which John speaks and also declares his own work as the fulfillment of that expectation. (Compare Matt. 11:5 with today's Old Testament lesson.) Jesus is to be recognized to the degree that he meets the messianic job description of the Hebrew Scriptures, and their value as a vehicle of the Word of God is seen in their testimony to him.

Early, then, in the liturgical year we are reminded of the importance of the Hebrew Scriptures for Christian worship. Marcionism, that early heresy that rejected the validity of the Old Testament, is still alive and well in many quarters. Its vitality is testified to by the large number of congregations where the Old Testament lectionary is rarely used, where the psalter as a book of devotion is ignored, and where Old Testament texts are rarely preached upon. Let nothing be said of teachers and preachers who still talk about the God of the Old Testament as a God of wrath and the God of the New Testament as a God of love!

Preachers should also receive from this text permission to preach Christ through the texts of the Old Testament. Historical sensitivity to the integrity of the Hebrew texts has frequently made modern preachers wary lest they make the prophets say more than they ever intended and, using Barth's image, end up finding Jesus hiding behind every rock in the Old Testament. Such historical sensitivity can be respected, however, without compromising the theological integrity

47

of the *sensus plenior* or the "fuller sense," in which Christians read those texts because of their experience with the risen Christ. Jesus of Nazareth, in today's lesson, does not say, "Yep, that was me that Isaiah was talking about." Rather he asks that parallels be drawn between Isaiah's hope and his own ministry. It is easy to see how simple-minded equations can be drawn. However, the preacher's task, among others, is to make clear that "the simple gospel isn't as simple as some simple people think." Creative preachers will think analogously between Hebrew and Christian scriptures in order to proclaim the God who is the source of both. It may be helpful to refer to the comments on this issue made under this section for the Second Sunday of Advent.

The Third Sunday of Advent has historically been called Gaudete Sunday, from the first word in the Latin introit for the day, "Rejoice in the Lord always; again I will say, Rejoice! . . . The Lord is near" (Phil. 4:4-5). See the opening essay for comments about the use of rose or pink on this day. Where compromises might be necessary in the observance of a strict Advent, the Old Testament lesson could guide us to this Sunday as the one for the hanging of the greens. An alternative rendering of the Old Testament lesson in this service might be from its arrangement in Handel's *Messiah*. A restrained celebration of Advent can be a vivid illustration of the practice of patience, as discussed in the epistle lesson. The whole tenor of the liturgy becomes an exercise in patience, the present work of the people of God. Our very worship helps us learn patience.

Fourth Sunday of Advent

Old Testament Texts

At the very heart of Advent is the anticipation and celebration of the incarnation—of God's being present with us. Our Old Testament lessons for the fourth week of Advent turn directly on this central theme. Isaiah 7:10-16 is a prophecy that anticipates Immanuel ("with us is God"), and Psalm 80 is a communal petition for God to be present.

The Lesson: *Isaiah 7:10-16*

The Sign of Immanuel

Setting. Isaiah 7:10-16 is a central Old Testament text for Christians. It was already given a central place in the formation of the Gospel of Matthew (where Isaiah 7:14 is quoted as a prophecy about the birth of Jesus), and it has continued to play a central role in our Advent worship throughout Christian history.

Toward the end of the eighth century B.C.E. a number of Judah's neighbors, including the northern kingdom of Israel (also known as Ephraim) and Syria, formed a coalition to fight against Assyria. Assyria was the major world power during this century, and the Syro-Ephraimite alliance was formed so that the smaller nations could maintain independence from this superpower. King Ahaz, the king of Judah, did not join the coalition, which weakened the potential strength of the alliance and prompted the Syrians and the Ephraimites to attack the southern kingdom of Judah. Judah was no match for such an alliance, and before long King Ahaz (the King of Judah) found himself under siege in Jerusalem probably around 735 B.C.E. (see II Kings 16:5-9 and II Chronicles 28:5-21). The seemingly immanent disaster that was closing in around King Ahaz and the entire southern

49

kingdom provides the historical setting for Isaiah's prophecy about Immanuel. Isaiah 7:1-2 tells us how the Syro-Ephraimite alliance "came up to attack Jerusalem to wage war against it," and that they had not yet conquered it. In addition, we are told that during this brief intermezzo, while Jerusalem is under siege but not yet quite conquered, Ahaz and all his people were terrified (they "shook as trees of the forest shake before the wind").

Such an attack on the southern kingdom was not only a political problem, it was also a religious problem. God had promised that a Davidic king would always rule (see the Second Sunday of Advent, Year A) and that God would dwell in the Temple in Jerusalem. These promises were not looking so good in the year 735 B.C.E. Was God really with the southern kingdom even during siege warfare? Isaiah the prophet certainly thought so, and he went to the king's pool to make his thoughts known to Ahaz. His political advice of pacificism in v. 4 ("Take heed, be quiet, do not fear") is rooted in his unwavering faith in God's messianic promise to be present with the people of God. As the messianic king, Ahaz had a special responsibility to embody this faith, for in fulfilling this role he was able to mediate divine blessing and well-being to the social order. It is the special messianic role of Ahaz that prompts Isaiah to conclude his first encounter with the king in v. 9 with the words, "If you do not stand firm in faith, you shall not stand at all."

Structure. The historical and literary setting of Isaiah 7 suggests that one should expand upon the lectionary, which has isolated vv. 10-16. These verses must function in the larger literary context of Isaiah 7:1-17. Note how v. 10 presupposes the earlier material by describing this encounter as an additional one and by assuming prophetic discourse without even mentioning Isaiah ("Again the LORD spoke to Ahaz."). Isaiah 7:1-17 separates into three parts: first, vv. 1-2 provide the historical context of the Syro-Ephraimite invasion of Judah; second, vv. 3-9 tell of the first encounter between the prophet Isaiah and King Ahaz at the Fuller's Field; and third, vv. 10-17 tell how the prophet encountered the king a second time.

Significance. Isaiah 7:10-17 is about divine signs of salvation during times of siege. The passage opens with Isaiah encouraging Ahaz to believe by testing God with a sign—any sign, big or small! The ability to test would confirm faith. Ahaz responds, however, in

v. 12 with pious religiosity that is meant to mask his unbelief, "I will not ask, and I will not put the LORD to the test." The text closes in vv. 13-17 with a prophetic sign meant to confirm the reliability of the messianic promises and unmask the king's unbelief.

The prophet's sign in vv. 13-17 acquires its meaning in the larger context of siege warfare. With the countryside already ransacked and the royal court eating the last of their stored food before starvation sets in, Isaiah gives a sign that affirms life in the midst of what appears to be certain death and destruction. He states that a young woman will actually give birth in the midst of this apparent death and starvation. The prophet's naming of the child provides interpretation: The birth of the child is a sign that "God is with us." The Immanuel sign goes beyond the birth to the land itself. Thus the prophet continues that before this child grows up he will be eating produce from the land. The sign is reliable because God is committed to the messianic promises.

The power of the Immanuel sign for Christians during Advent is that it calls us to live faithfully in God's promise to be with us and indeed even to have the courage of faith to test that promise when we are under siege.

Such times of siege may be intellectual, spiritual, or sociopolitical. They occur when we no longer believe that God is able to reverse threatening situations that confront us, even while we mask our unbelief in pious clichés. One example is when the power of a skeptical age forces us to cover up our unbelief in a personal God through complex God-talk that, in the end, demands nothing of the diety. Another example is when we concede inherited roles of the oppressed and the oppressor, even while we bemoan the evil results of such structures. The power of the Immanual sign is that all evil structures can be reversed. The challenge of the Immanuel sign is stated by the prophet to King Ahaz in v. 9, "If you do not stand firm in faith, you shall not stand at all."

The Response: *Psalm 80:1-7, 17-19*

A Communal Petition for God to Be Present

Setting. Psalm 80:1-7, 17-19 bears the marks of a worship liturgy. Note the refrain that occurs in vv. 3, 7, 19. The psalm, therefore, was probably read by a worship leader or priest, with the congregation answering by means of the refrains. The refrain, with its request for God to break through to the worshiping community and save them, provides insight into the genre of this hymn as a communal or national lament during a time of stress. The reference to Ephraim, Benjamin, and Manasseh in v. 2 has prompted scholars to locate this psalm in the northern kingdom sometime before its fall in 722 B.C.E.

Structure. The refrains provide clear markers for separating the psalm into three parts: vv. 1-3, 4-7, and 17-19. Section one is a plea for help; section two raises the question of how long God will remain angry with the people of God; and section three is a promise that if God comes to the aid of his people, they will remain faithful to God. All three sections conclude with the congregation joining in with a petition for salvation.

Significance. The lament of Psalm 80:1-7, 18-19 provides a fitting conclusion to Advent and a transition to Christmas. First, the divine imagery in the psalm anticipates two central figures of God that we associate with Christmas: the enthroned God in the Temple and the shepherd. The imagery of God enthroned in the Temple emphasizes divine eminence that we associate with the incarnation, and the imagery of God as a shepherd, underscores the close relationship that we have with God as we are led through life. Second, the lament with its anticipation of the appearance of God mirrors the situation of worshipers at the close of Advent. We wait with anticipation for the appearance of God at Christmas. Finally, we experience anew the call for salvation that is rooted in confidence which arises out of the past acts of God's salvation (v. 1).

New Testament Texts

The worship leader confronts an embarrassment of riches in the texts for the final Sunday of Advent, Year A. Both readings reflect upon Jesus' divine sonship, though in different ways: Romans in terms of Jesus' descent, titles, and resurrection; Matthew in terms of virginal (or pneumatic) conception and Jesus' name. The passage from Romans and the one from Matthew are concerned with Jesus'

identity, and both texts articulate the role of Jesus in the operation
of God's salvation.

The Epistle: *Romans 1:1-7*

Grasping the Gospel of God

Setting. These verses form the salutation of Paul's letter to the
Christian community in Rome. The apostle did not found that fellowship of believers, and he had never visited the group. Yet, he
writes to them expressing concern about the future of his ministry,
especially because he hopes to spend time among the Romans as he
moves toward Spain as his next mission field. In the normal fashion of
his letters Paul identifies both himself and those to whom he writes in
terms of their new identities, which have been formed in relationship
to God and Christ. In this particular greeting, Paul speaks elaborately
(perhaps incorporating words from an early Christian confession),
probably because he wants his own comprehension of their mutual
faith to be clear to the Roman Christians.

Structure. Paul's theme is "the gospel of God." He speaks of
God's good news in three ways: (1) God's gospel was given as
promise; (2) it was brought to fulfillment in God's Son, who is related
to God's past (the time of the promise) in terms of his heritage (Son of
David) and who is the locus of God's power demonstrated in the
Resurrection; and (3) it means the establishment of Jesus Christ as the
Lord of the Christian community that experiences grace and receives a
commission to ministry.

Significance. Paul identifies himself and his work in relation to his
call in these opening verses of Romans, but it would be a mistake to
focus on the person of Paul when using this passage for preaching and
worship. Rather, Paul's theme, "the gospel of God," must occupy
those who work with this text; and it is wise to allow the apostle's own
remarks to direct contemporary reflection on this text.

First, the "good news" of which Paul speaks is not merely a
message about God; it is God's own good news. This is evident in
Paul's phrase *the gospel of God*—which, as the theme of the rest of the
letter to the Romans shows, is a subjective genitive construction—

meaning "God's gospel." Thus the good news is neither human innovation nor human insight or conclusion. Furthermore, as Paul says, God's good news was promised beforehand through the prophets and recorded in Holy Scripture. God takes initiative in actualizing the promise, but as God acts, already humans have been given the standard of scripture for evaluating the validity of the claims of the gospel message. While the news for us these days may be that God is the one who accomplishes God's purposes, not us, at the same time, we should see that we are called into the operation of God's promise-keeping at the first level, for not all claims about God will wash with scripture, which serves to guide our thinking about God. Paul does not assume that the Romans are passive listeners with empty heads. Rather, he assumes a congregation that cares enough to be informed and involved with the good news.

Second, the gospel message is not merely any old message. God's gospel has to do specifically with God's Son, who is himself the complete fulfillment of God's promises. This connection is indicated in the reference to Jesus' descent from David according to the flesh. Notice, however, that God's power is present in an unprecedented fashion in the fulfillment of God's promise in Jesus Christ. The Resurrection makes clear that Jesus is the Son of God in power, and it reveals the true character of God's power, which is power perfected and manifested in the context of weakness. Remember, the one raised from the dead in demonstration of the power of God was he who fulfilled God's promise in a life of service that moved to a gruesome death on a Roman cross. We comprehend the power of God as we see it operate in the Resurrection of the crucified one.

Third, the promise of God fulfilled in Jesus Christ has essential meaning for our existence. We experience grace as a result of God's work in Jesus Christ, specifically because the power of God that raised Jesus has made him the Lord of the Christian community. Jesus Christ is the one whose will directs the lives of believers; so that for us, life under the Lordship of Christ is an experience of grace! This grace is not merely a privilege to possess and ponder; rather, the gift of grace in faith means a life of obedience that ultimately involves us all in the doing of Christian ministry.

The Gospel: *Matthew 1:18-25*

God's Action and Our Reactions

Setting. Matthew begins his version of the story of Jesus Christ with a lengthy genealogy of Jesus. That catalogue of "begats" serves to trace the people of God from Abraham to David through the Babylonian exile to Jesus, but Matthew is persuaded and insists that the symmetry of the history shows the hand of God, not a mere chronological ramble. Immediately after the genealogy and Matthew's comments on it comes the story of the birth of Jesus. The Gospel lesson for this week is the first subunit in the larger story. This opening incident establishes the exceptional nature of the story as a whole.

Structure. Verses 18-25 have three movements. First, verses 18-21 tell of the divine conception of Jesus, Joseph's reservations, and the initial appearance and instructions of the angel to Joseph. Second, vv. 22-23 give a two-layered interpretation: Matthew explains the events in relation to Old Testament scripture and then provides a clarification of the Old Testament text (Isaiah 7:14). Third, Matthew takes up the story again and reports the outcome of Joseph's nocturnal visitation.

Furthermore, within these three movements there is another four-part internal structure related to Matthew's sequence. First, there is the conception with attendant human doubt and divine confirmation; second, there is a commissioning of Joseph by the angel; third, there is commentary from Matthew relating the events to the text of Isaiah; and fourth, there is the report of Joseph's compliance with the angelic commission.

Significance. With the story of Jesus' conception, Matthew clearly tells us that at a particular time, in a particular place, in a particular way, in the life of a particular person, God intervened in history in order to accomplish the salvation of humanity. For citizens of a modern, scientifically oriented world, the idea of Jesus' conception by the Holy Spirit and the virgin Mary is often hard to comprehend. For most people there are doubts (unless one simply puts all questions on hold). Remarkably, in this story Joseph himself has doubts; we see that (1) such reservations are nothing new and (2) those who today have reservations are in good company.

Notice also that Joseph's doubts are answered by divine confirmation of the extraordinary conditions of Jesus' conception. Few persons today who have difficulties with the virginal/pneumatic conception of Jesus have reported a personal visit from an angel to assuage their reservations. To expect such a visit may be an inappropriate hope, for the story is about God's intervention through Jesus and his place in God's work for the saving of the world. In other words, the story carries a message much larger and greater than the mere notion of virginal/pneumatic conception—the story declares the gracious love of God that reaches into the context of human existence in an unprecedented fashion through Jesus Christ to do for us humans what we cannot do for ourselves.

The angel assures Joseph of the situation and God's involvement in Mary's pregnancy, but the angel does more than relieve Joseph's mind. Joseph gets a crucial commission; he is to give the name Jesus to the child that Mary will bear. With a relieved mind, Joseph is given a job to do. For the ancient Jews a name was an expression of one's fundamental nature, not merely a label. To name the child Jesus is to state that he achieves the salvation that Israel anticipated from God; to call the baby Jesus is to say that this Spirit-born baby is the one who "will save his people from their sins" (1:22). Notice at this story's end (vv. 24-25) that Joseph is faithful and obedient in doing the task he is given.

Matthew is concerned that the readers understand that the saving work of God in Jesus is divine intervention, but he also writes to make clear that the salvation accomplished through Jesus Christ is no pure innovation. Matthew declares that the conception of Jesus is a fulfillment of scripture. This idea is crucial for Matthew, for he understands and presents Jesus throughout the Gospel as the one in whom all the expectations of Israel, expressed in scripture, are fulfilled. While making this point, Matthew scores a profound theological note when he cites Isaiah 7:14. That text refers to the naming of a child called "Emmanuel," which Matthew tells us means "God with us." Why mention "Emmanuel" when talking about

Jesus? In shorthand Matthew is saying that Jesus saves his people by being God with us. The importance of this understanding of the person and work of Jesus colors the entire Gospel which moves to its concluding scene on a mountain in Galilee where the risen Jesus Christ promises, ''And remember, I am with you always, to the close of the age'' (28:20b).

Advent 4: The Celebration

Much like a movie ''flashback,'' Advent comes at last to the beginning of the story! Today we prepare for Christmas, but unlike every other birth, we know a great deal about this child in advance. We began the season by learning of his eschatological identity and then moved back into history to consider him as the fulfillment of Israel's messianic expectation as proclaimed after his birth by John the Baptist. We then jumped ahead a few months to hear Jesus talking about John and testifying to the truth of that proclamation. Now we are preparing to hear how it was that all this had come about. Notice that it is still preparation; in the Gospel for today we are still preparing for Jesus' birth. In some ways, this structure of Advent matches the experience of the early Christians. They were waiting for Christ's final triumph because they had experienced his ministry as a sign of God's faithfulness, and while they waited they told the story of how it had all come about. ''It took place in this way. . . .'' Waiting and celebration, rejoicing and recitation, go hand in hand. The liturgical planner's job is to tell the story so that the hearers are anxious for what comes next.

The pastor will be sorely tempted to indulge in a riot of Christmas carols on this day because of the pervasiveness of the secular culture and its tendency to alter time for its own convenience (as with President's Day, for example). For that reason the temptation should be resisted. Still, some traditional music is appropriate for this liturgy. An examination of what the text of a hymn is really saying should help determine its appropriateness. ''Joy to the World, the Lord is Come'' is a general fact that makes the hymn usable at almost any time of the year, especially Christmas. ''It Came upon the Midnight Clear'' is a recalling of what we will be celebrating later in the week. On the other hand, "Silent Night, Holy Night, all is calm" and "born this happy morning" suggest that certain times are more significant for their use.

Psalm 80 replaces the traditional use of Psalm 24 on this Sunday. It might be best to ignore the new usage of Psalm 80 and continue the former usage of Psalm 24. Psalm 24 suggests the use of "Lift Up Your Heads, Ye Mighty Gates." Those churches that sing antiphons to introduce and conclude the psalm might use the last two lines of the first stanza to serve this function. This hymn as printed in *The United Methodist Hymnal* (No. 213) could serve as a leitmotif throughout the service by using the entire hymn for the opening, stanza 2 could be a call to prayer by the choir, and stanza 3 could be the people's response either immediately or at the conclusion of the prayers. If stanza 3 were not used here, it could be sung as the acclamation after the institution narrative in the Great Thanksgiving. Stanza 4 could serve as a response to the benediction. Thus the hymn could serve as a chain holding the elements of the service together. Because the text varies between hymnals, pastors and musicians will need to see how their particular version could be employed.

The following is a little-known Christmas hymn of Charles Wesley, which has not appeared in American hymnals for over a hundred years. The language makes it an excellent commentary on today's Gospel, and the congregation or a soloist could sing it to the familiar tune Darwall's 148th (no. 715 in *The United Methodist Hymnal* and no. 155 in *The Presbyterian Hymnal*). It is appropriate for today and any time throughout Christmas. If preferred, the first three stanzas could be used as an independent unit.

> Let earth and heaven combine,
> Angels and men agree,
> To praise in songs divine
> The incarnate Deity,
> Our God contracted to a span,
> Incomprehensibly made man.
>
> He laid his glory by,
> He wrapped him in our clay;
> Unmarked by human eye,
> The latent Godhead lay;
> Infant of days he here became,
> And bore the mild Immanuel's name.

Unsearchable the love
That has the Savior brought;
The grace is far above
Or men or angels' thought:
Suffice for us that God, we know,
Our God, is manifest below.

He deigns in flesh to appear,
Widest extremes to join;
To bring our vileness near,
And make us all divine:
And we the life of God shall know,
For God is manifest below.

Made perfect first in love,
And sanctified by grace,
We shall from earth remove,
And see his glorious face:
His love shall then be fully showed,
And we shall all be lost in God.

Even if not used in worship, the preacher could do worse than meditate on this hymn daily during Advent as a preparation for preaching at Christmas!

THE PASCHAL MYSTERY AND CHRISTMAS/EPIPHANY

Those who were trained in the old "pie chart" understanding of the Christian year may be a bit surprised to discover that the new calendar speaks of Christmas/Epiphany, with January 6 being the last day of Christmas, rather than the first day of a new season. The reason for this change is actually a return to the origins of both festivals, Christmas and Epiphany, and a recognition that the division of the two into separate seasons was really the result of Western chauvinism. Epiphany, the older of the two festivals, originated in the East and celebrated both the birth and the baptism of Jesus. It also emphasized the mystery of the Incarnation as central to understanding these events. Christmas, as a feast of the nativity in particular, developed later in Rome. Some have maintained that December 25 was chosen to compete with the cult of Mithra which celebrated the birth of its sun god on that day. Others suggest more complicated reasons having to do with dating back from what was believed to have been the date of the Crucifixion.

December 25 won out in the Western church as the date for celebrating the birth of Jesus. Because January 6 had been so important earlier, it was retained, but the emphasis on Epiphany, the manifestation of God in the world, was reduced to the visit of the wise men, who were pictured as being of three races, so as to symbolize the whole world. The races were rarely ever pictured as including Caucasians, giving the impression that only "colored peoples" were in need of missionary outreach! In American Protestantism, this was to become the rationale for turning the season of Epiphany into a programmatic occasion emphasizing missions. Visiting missionaries combed the countrysides during the worst weather of the year in faithfulness to the pie chart, and confirmation classes were taught that green was the color of the season because it symbolized the growth of the church through missionary activity! The difficulty with this approach is not so much that it is misleading but that it is so limited in its understanding of mission. The church's mission grows not out of the visit of the Magi, but out of the whole work of Christ, and therefore mission is an appropriate topic at any time, because it is the reason for the church's existence. The Western church's particular emphasis also led to an eclipse of the baptism of Jesus and its commemoration.

The result of all this history is that the new calendar observes a festival of the Incarnation and Manifestation from December 25 through January 6, Christmas through Epiphany. It then observes time "after Epiphany," or, in some traditions, "ordinary time." The First Sunday After Epiphany is The Baptism of the Lord, thus bringing that event into prominence once more.

Another difficulty with referring to the visit of the Magi as "the Epiphany" in such an exclusive way is that it ignores the fact that the Gospels are rich in epiphanies. The intent of the Gospels is to be an epiphany by recording "all that Jesus began to do and to teach." Having celebrated the birth of Jesus at Christmas/Epiphany, the time after Epiphany is spent examining who this is who has come among us. Each year the last Sunday after Epiphany, regardless of how many Sundays there may be, is the Sunday of the Transfiguration. This is the epiphany that begins the chain of events leading to Jesus' death and Resurrection (Gospel, Year C).

So it is the Paschal mystery that finally enables us to interpret Christmas and Epiphany. The Gospel writers constantly report the amazement or lack of comprehension that accompanies Jesus' ministry; understanding comes only by the light of the Resurrection. As we do not celebrate Advent by pretending that Christ has not come, so we do not celebrate Christmas by pretending that we don't know what is going to happen to this child. Christmas cannot be celebrated properly in isolation from the rest of the Christ-event. To separate the story of Jesus' birth from the harsh reality of the crucifixion is to engage in a pious fraud, a sentimental blasphemy. Careful exegesis of the lessons for the time will make evident the opportunities the scripture gives to relate incarnation and atonement, the cradle and the cross.

Because Epiphany Day will usually fall during the week, the lectionary gives the option of substituting it and its lessons on the First Sunday After Christmas. Provided January 6 falls later than the Second Sunday After Christmas it could also be observed on that day. The reason for this is that the First Sunday After Epiphany is always The Baptism of the Lord, thus giving priority to an event which is attested to by all the Gospels. Because of space limitations, this volume will discuss only the propers for the Sundays after Christmas and will comment on the Epiphany Day propers in the Year B volume.

The Services of Christmas

The Western Catholic tradition has observed three services for Christmas Day: one at midnight, one at dawn, and one during the day. That accounts for the three propers listed in the lectionary. Because of space, this series will deal with one proper each year. The lessons remain the same for all three years, and worship planners may exercise the option of changing the lessons around between the services. This is encouraged in the case of the Gospel reading for the service during the day, the Johannine prologue, if there is a chance that it will be omitted otherwise. For those who wish to use John 1 this year, see the exegetical comment on pages 95-97, where it also appears as the Gospel reading for the Second Sunday After Christmas.

The pattern in much of American Protestantism is to have one or two earlier services followed by a midnight service on Christmas Eve, and only in rare instances are services held on Christmas Day. Usually the earlier service is a "family" or "children's" service. The set of three propers in the lectionary can be adapted very easily to this tradition, particularly since the Gospel reading for the first two propers are the familiar Christmas story from Luke.

If there is a crèche in the church, the placing of the figure of Jesus in the manger might take place after the reading of Luke 2:7. This could be accompanied by the singing of one or more stanzas of "Away in a Manger" and the use of the following unison prayer:

> Lord Jesus,
>   I offer to you
>   the gold of my love,
>   the incense of my prayers,
>   the myrrh of my willingness to bear the cross.
>   Amen.

The service would then continue with the reading of the Gospel. For those who object to such an interruption of the Gospel reading, this brief devotion can be used as an entrance rite at the beginning of the service, with the image of Jesus being brought in during the procession.

Christmas is a popular time for "candlelight services," and they are often advertised in such a way as to give the impression that the candlelight is an end in itself rather than a rich symbol of what the birth of Christ means to the world. Attention to the Paschal character of our worship will always help us guard against a manipulated sentimental religiosity. Ideally, the Advent wreath, with its function of "counting down" to Christmas, should disappear before the first service of the season. If it has come equipped with a "Christ candle," light only that candle for these services of Christmas Eve/Day. After that it should vanish, so as not to give the impression that it is on an equal footing with the Paschal candle, which is the primary light in the church symbolizing the presence of Christ. Again, it is the Paschal symbol that takes priority and gives meaning to what we are doing, even at Christmas.

Where the service involves all the members of the congregation having lighted candles, take care that directions are clear, brief, and to the point. The effect of the occasion is diminished if the pastor is constantly giving warnings about dropping wax on the new carpet! Imaginative worship planners should think about how a service can be a "candlelight" service without having to put live flames in the hands of everyone present.

The midnight service is most appropriately eucharistic, and that emphasis should not be overshadowed by any candlelighting exercise, a case of bad liturgy driving out good. Christmas is the celebration of the Incarnation, the scandalous proclamation that God took on human flesh and blood. The elements of bread and wine remind us of this "materialistic" character of God who comes to meet us again in the Eucharist, a symbol of Christ incarnate.

Just as the services of Advent have been characterized by reserve and a sense of anticipation, so also the services of Christmas unleash a torrent of praise and adoration through word, music, and visuals. Avoid clutter in both chancel and nave to allow for adequate liturgical movement. If live Christmas trees are used, let them be in proportion to the space, and, hopefully, potted, so that later they can be planted as a sign of ecological responsibility. Give some thought as to whether they are decorated or left bare. Candles and flowers should point to the Lord's Table, neither camouflaging it nor making it difficult to set for the Eucharist. The church's celebratory colors of white and/or gold are used during this time.

Christmas Day, First Proper (Christmas Eve/Christmas Day)

Old Testament Texts

Many of the Advent themes reappear in the Christmas Eve lessons as present realities rather than as future hopes. Isaiah 9:2-9 picks up the imagery of the light of Zion that was hoped for in Isaiah 2:1-5 and turns it into a present time celebration, while Psalm 96 does the same thing with the royal theology of Isaiah 11:1-10. Taken together our Old Testament lessons describe the new reality that God ushers into our world.

The Lesson: *Isaiah 9:2-7*

Seeing the Light

Setting. Isaiah 9:2-7 is a prophetic hymn of thanksgiving. The text celebrates a radical reversal in the fortunes of Israel through the imagery of light and darkness in v. 2. Even though the people once walked in darkness, they are presently experiencing a "great light." Scholars debate the historical circumstances in the life of the prophet Isaiah that would have given rise to this celebration, and whether this text is related to the prophecy to King Ahaz in Isaiah 7:10-16, which was our text for the Fourth Sunday of Advent. These issues cannot be resolved here. Most important for using this text on Christmas is that we see the roots of this celebration in Israel's royal theology, and more specifically how this theology is grounded in grace—namely, that God is faithful to divine promises.

Structure. The hymn of thanksgiving separates into three parts: opening praise to God (vv. 2-3), reasons for praising God (vv. 4-7*a*), and concluding assurance (v. 7*b*).

Significance. The praise to God in vv. 2-3 centers on the image of light. This motif inaugurated the Advent season with the eschatological vision of Zion in Isaiah 2:1-5, where the prophet encouraged Israel to walk in the light of God even while the people looked to the future for its full brilliance. In Isaiah 9:2 the full brilliance of the light is a present reality to be celebrated in the here and now. In v. 3 we learn that the light is a sign of God's presence with the people of God and that it is a reason for joy, but we do not yet know what activity of God is signified by the light.

The reasons for praise in vv. 4-7a include three present activities of God that make up the light. The three divine actions are indicated with the word *for* at the beginning of vv. 4, 5, 6. Each action fills out the content of the light and in so doing provides a cause for celebration. The first two actions are violent images about the breaking in of salvation, while the third begins to sketch out contours of a new world that is emerging because God's salvation is already present.

First, v. 4 describes the salvation of God as a radical reversal in the structure of earthly power through the imagery of holy war. Salvation, as the result of a divine holy war against human power structures, was the central way in which biblical writers tried to give content to what the presence of God in this world really means. The Exodus, for example, is presented to the reader as a holy war between God, whose presence in Egypt unleashes new and strange notions of power, and Pharaoh, the epitome of human power. Isaiah 9:4 provides its own historical reference to holy war when we are told that God has overturned the oppressor as "on the day of Midian." The story of Gideon in Judges 6–9 provides an excellent example of divine holy war for two reasons. First, it illustrates how the breaking in of God's salvation into this world necessarily creates conflict between different kinds of power; in this case, the Midianites against Israel. Second, it underscores how salvation, or victory in this holy war, can come only from God. Even though Gideon, the main character in this story, started out to fight the Midianites with a large force of well-armed soldiers, by the time he reaches the Midianite camp his force is reduced to three hundred, and they have only jars and trumpets for weapons.

Second, v. 5 takes the holy war imagery even further. The prophet tells us that the defeat of the powers which stand over against God will be permanent. Blood-stained garments of war will be burned up.

Third, vv. 6-7a are a celebration of the birth of a messianic king, who embodies the new salvific power that God has unleashed in the world through holy war. Verse 6 describes the quality of this messianic king, while v. 7a describes the character of his rule. The quality of the king is sketched out with traditional throne names: "Wonderful Counselor" (a prudent ruler), "Mighty God" (one capable of carrying on God's holy war of salvation), "Everlasting Father" (one who will rule for a long time and provide protection), "Prince of Peace" (one who is able to transmit divine blessing to the social order). The character of this king's rule is justice, righteousness, and everlasting peace.

The hymn of thanksgiving ends in v. 7a where it began by celebrating the reliability of salvation because God is faithful to his divine promises.

Isaiah 9:2-9 is a familiar text for worship at Christmas. We especially like to focus on the third reason for praise, namely the birth of the messianic child. And so we should. By looking at the larger context of Isaiah 9:2-7, we learn, however, that the birth of the child in Isaiah 9:6-7a takes place in the setting of holy war and is not about a romantic manger scene. God's breaking into our world through incarnation unleashes a new kind of power that will inevitably put us in conflict with all human notions of power and security. It is this new power freely given to us that we celebrate at Christmas. In doing this at Christmas, we, like Israel at the time of Isaiah, see the light and participate in God's holy war of justice and righteousness. This holy war may be waged within the intimacy of our churches or in the larger sociopolitical context of the nations. On whatever level we find ourselves participating in holy war, Christmas is God's revelation that our risk is divinely shared.

The Response: *Psalm 96*

Singing a New Song

Setting. Psalm 96 is an enthronement psalm. The ancient Israelites used enthronement psalms in special liturgies to celebrate the unique presence of God with Israel in the Temple and God's kingship over all creation. The presence of God was probably symbolized in the worship service by means of the ark of the covenant, which would be carried into the Temple with a processional and placed in the Holy of Holies. The placing of the ark in the sanctuary provided the occasion for Israel to celebrate liturgically the reality that God was present in this world and that "The Lord reigns!" (Psalm 96:10). Thus this is a most appropriate psalm for a Christmas service in which we celebrate the presence of God in our world through the Incarnation.

Structure. Psalm 96 can be divided between vv. 1-6 and 7-13, with each section following the same two-part structure. Verses 1-6 are a call for the worshiping community to praise God. Verses 1-3 exhort those present to sing a new song, and in so doing to bless God's name and tell of his salvation. Verses 4-6 provide the reasons for praise (notice the word *for* in vv. 4, 5). God is great, God is to be feared, God is the creator, and so on. Verses 7-13 are a call for all people to praise God. Verses 7-9 encourage "the families of the people" to worship God, while vv. 10-13 describe how God rules all aspects of creation and will judge all people.

Significance. Isaiah 9:2-7 provides excellent background for interpreting Psalm 96. Both texts celebrate God's presence in this world and the reliability of God's power to rule. The imagery of holy war in Isaiah 9:4-5 is very important, because it provides content to the "new song" that the people of God are being encouraged to sing in Psalm 96:1. Psalm 96 is a celebration of power, but it is not the kind of power that we are most familiar with and comfortable with. Indeed, the psalmist tells us in v. 5 that our status quo notions of power ("the gods of the peoples") are of no account ("idols"), because "the Lord reigns" (v. 10). The new song of this psalm is possible because God has been victorious in a holy war against our notions of power and security, has unleashed a new form of power for our salvation, and now rules our world with righteousness and truth (v. 13). Christmas is a celebration of this enthronement of God, which evokes a semipacifistic approach to overcoming worldly power.

New Testament Texts

The declaration in the opening line of the text from Titus (at first glance a seemingly odd text for Christmas) summarizes the essence of both New Testament readings: "For the grace of God has appeared—salvation to all persons" (author's translation). The development of this theme is handled differently in Titus and Luke, but the shared subject and the relating of this declaration to Jesus Christ bind these very different texts to each other for use on Christmas.

The Epistle: *Titus 2:11-14*

The Practical Meaning of Salvation

Setting. The letter to Titus is designed to give advice to a Christian leader who is facing a less than perfect pastoral situation. The letter gives counsel about the personal qualities a pastor is to possess (1:5-9), and then it provides directions for dealing with those in the church who create problems (1:10-16). Next, the letter admonishes the pastor to teach sound doctrine and lays out standards for different types of believers—older men, older women, younger women, younger men, and slaves (2:1-10). The reading for this Sunday delineates the essence of the meaning of salvation. Then, 2:15 concludes the section on Christian teaching, saying, "Declare these things; exhort and reprove with all authority. Let no one look down on you."

Structure. The text opens declaring salvation by grace. It then reflects upon both what is inappropriate and what is appropriate for the lives of believers. The current Christian disposition of waiting (similar to the theme of Advent) is mentioned before the text ends by explaining briefly the substance of Christ's saving work.

Significance. Grace, according to these verses, means salvation, and salvation brings a definite kind of living. First, in the present, a steady transformation occurs in the lives of believers, so that they deliberately move away from impiety and worldly passions (literally, "worldly lusts"). Doing away with such inappropriate attitudes and practices is not, however, merely putting on a facade of piety, for growth away from impiety and worldly lusts is the result of the operation of grace in the lives of the believers. It is not that we are saved and, therefore, we must act a certain way; rather, it is that saving grace is active in our lives and we are being freed from ungodliness. Furthermore, our freedom is not only freedom from; it is also freedom for. As we grow away from unholy manners of living, we grow toward moderation, righteousness, and devotion. These dimensions of our existence as Christians are the results of God's gracious work in our lives. Thus, in the present, grace yields salvation and that means the negation of some characteristics of our being and creation of others.

Christian living has a present, but it also has a future. Titus 2:13 reminds us that we live awaiting our hope: "the manifestation of the glory of our great God and Savior, Jesus Christ." While Christmas comes after Advent and reminds us of the present reality of grace, which came in the historical figure of Jesus Christ, we must not conclude that the full purposes of God have already been achieved. Salvation is presently real, but grace is still working to achieve even more of God's will. We celebrate the reality of transforming grace, but we also hope for the fullest form of God's salvation.

Finally, Titus 2:14 makes christologically clear everything written in the preceding verses. Referring to the person and work of our Savior Jesus Christ, this verse relates his selfless self-giving to the notions of freedom from and freedom for by stating that Christ "gave himself for us that he might redeem us from all iniquity and to purify for himself a people of his own who are zealous for good deeds."

The Gospel: *Luke 2:1-20*

The Surprising Shape of Salvation

Setting. Luke 1–2 is Luke's version of the story of Jesus' birth. The account is set in a highly dramatic and intensely Jewish environment, though anyone reading or hearing Luke's story must take into account that the religious world of Judaism was part of a larger Greco-

Roman political world. The narrative is quite deliberately formed, because Luke tells the story of the birth of Jesus in such a way that the annunciation, birth, circumcision, and naming of John the Baptist precede and alternate with the same kinds of events in the life of Jesus. In Luke 1:5-25 the birth of John is foretold, and in Luke 1:26-38 the forthcoming birth of Jesus is announced. Then, Luke 1:57-66 tells of the birth, circumcision, and naming of John; and later, Luke 2:1-21 narrates the birth, circumcision, and naming of Jesus.

Structure. The text for this Sunday falls naturally into three parts: Luke 2:1-7 tells of the census and Jesus' birth; 2:8-14 recounts the encounter of the shepherds and the angels; and 2:15-20 relates the visit of the shepherds to the holy family. One may use the text as one grand triptych, or one may select one or two of the panels for preaching and worship.

Significance. (A) The opening verses (2:1-7) score a number of points. The beginning of the section which mentions the powers-that-were in the Greco-Roman world locates the holy family in the context of a momentarily peaceful, but ever politically volatile, world. The mention of Bethlehem, named as the city of David, sets the Jewish world over against the Roman dominated political situation as it recalls the former glories of Israel. At the same time, for one in the know, the mention of Bethlehem, the city of David, would immediately conjure up thoughts of the promise of God to David that his heir would one day reign in peaceful glory. The world into which Jesus was born was at peace, but it was Caesar's peace, a human peace, and not the promised peace of God that comes through God's gracious work.

Having conjured up shades of traditional Davidic expectations, Luke moves to recount the birth of Jesus. He tells the story so that the humble circumstances of Jesus' birth are accentuated. Jesus is born in a stable and laid in a manger because there is no room for his parents (despite Mary's obvious condition) in the normal lodging facilities; though the world had Caesar's peace, it was still far from perfect. Despite the modest accommodations, Jesus' parents demonstrate great care by wrapping their child neatly in the approved manner of the day. Nevertheless, one should not forget that the conditions of the world and Joseph and Mary's limited means preclude Jesus' birth taking place in conditions of great comfort. At root Luke is emphasizing the genuine humility of Jesus' family: He was not born into power, privilege, or pleasure; instead he arrived in plebeian surroundings adorned only with parental love.

The majestic and imaginative language of this passage invites the responsible use of one's homiletical imagination. For example, the mention of Jesus' being laid in the manger suggests his role as the saving food of the world (this is my body; this is my blood—for you). And the memory that there was no room in the inn for Mary, Joseph, and the babe-about-to-be foreshadows the actual reception that Jesus encountered as he lived and worked in the course of his ministry.

(B) The ensuing verses (8-14) introduce the shepherds, who are appropriate characters given the location in the city of David. Some scholars suggest that the shepherds were employees of the Temple, assigned to take care of the animals designated; but the precise identification of these characters is not crucial. Rather, again, Luke accentuates the humility of the situation of Jesus' birth. In Caesar's world, God did not send Jesus Christ to the courts of kings, queens, and the rulers of this earth; instead he was born in a stable, and the good news was first proclaimed to common shepherds on the night shift.

Notice the shepherds' reaction to the appearance of the angel: they feared a great fear! It may be that Luke means to indicate the shepherds' piety with this report, so that "fear" is "fear of the Lord," but nothing in the text makes this plain. It is more likely that the glory of the angels evoked a sheer passivity on the part of the shepherds who were simply awed by the event. Yet, notice, too, that the shepherds are not left in the grips of fear; they are called out of their fright as the angel proclaims the good news, which becomes a sign to which they are to attend. Inherent in the good news of God's grace is a calling to action.

One should not overlook the deep irony at the heart of the angel's declaration. God has given the world a Savior, Christ the Lord, and the arrival of this Savior is the cause for great joy. But the Savior is a baby, born in humble circumstances that both contrast with and reveal the true character of God's power and glory. And so, the angels sing—proclaiming God's glory, which results in the true peace of the world.

(C) In the final verses of the reading (15-20), we see that curiosity did not kill the cat of the nighttime shepherds of Bethlehem. No sooner had the angels departed than the shepherds turned to investigate the good news! Being told about God's saving grace produced action in the lives of the shepherds. What they did about the care of the flock is anybody's guess, but clearly they moved swiftly to see the highly acclaimed baby with their own eyes.

For those viewing this text with homiletical eyes, the various actions of the characters are remarkable. On the one hand, Mary experienced the results of the operation of grace and meditated on the events. On the other hand, in the shepherds we see the second evangelists. (The angels were the first.) Having seen the baby, they set out to spread the good news, and their own proclamations now produced wonder among those who heard the story. Moreover, notice that the shepherds are not suddenly made celebrities by having had a visit from the angels and by having seen God's Savior. Far from getting swollen heads, the shepherds focused away from themselves, first, by sharing the good news, and second, by worshiping God!

Christmas Eve/Christmas Day: The Celebration

This set of lessons is designed for the first worship service of Christmas, usually the midnight service, the bridge service between Advent and Christmas. This explains the tone of the Old Testament lesson and psalm, recalling earlier Advent themes as they do, and the knitting together of both themes in the epistle where it is proclaimed that "the grace of God has appeared," but that we are still "awaiting . . . the appearing of . . . Jesus Christ." With that backward and forward look to the First Sunday of Advent, the Gospel lesson then sets us squarely in the Christmas celebration.

The abundance of liturgical resources for Christmas demands great discretion from worship planners and an acknowledgment that everything cannot be packed into one service. It is important to remember that there are other days of Christmas to come! If these lessons are used for a children's or family service earlier on Christmas Eve, the reading of the Gospel can provide the context for the Christmas pageant or tableau that is customary in many churches. Bringing the Christ Child to the crèche was discussed earlier on p. 63. The metrical paraphrase of the Old Testament lesson, "The people that in darkness sat" (*The Methodist Hymnal* [1964], no. 361) is fitting as a choral introit just before a candlelight procession. For churches that observe the ancient custom of not using the "Gloria in excelsis" (Glory be to God on high) during Advent, or that have never used it, tonight is the time for it to be heard again in anticipation of the angels' song in the Gospel. The choir's Christmas gift to the congregation could be learning this ancient hymn in one of its many settings. Traditionally it is used early in the service, but on this occasion it might serve as a response to the reading of the Gospel.

Throughout all the services of Christmas, this stanza from "As with Gladness Men of Old" (tune, Dix) can be a welcome substitute to the doxology at the presentation of the offering.

> As they offered gifts most rare
> At that manger rude and bare,
> So may we with holy joy,
> Pure and free from sin's alloy,
> All our costliest treasures bring,
> Christ, to thee, our heav'nly King.

The ethical significance of the epistle is whimsically caught up in Martin Luther's commentary on the Gospel in a way that is at once humbling and challenging to us. The sum of it is here:

"Unto you is born this day . . . . a Saviour." Let us look for a moment at the spiritual significance. Mary is the figure of Christianity, that is, all Christians who wrap the newborn Child in the word of the Gospel. The swaddling clothes signify the preaching of the Gospel; the manger signifies the place where Christians come together to hear the word of God. The ox and the ass stand for us. "And the shepherds returned, glorifying and praising God for all the things that they had heard and seen, as it was told unto them." This is wrong. We should correct this passage to read, "They went and shaved their heads, fasted, told their rosaries, and put on cowls." Instead we read, "The shepherds returned." Where to? To their sheep. Oh, that can't be right! Did they not leave everything and follow Christ? Must not one forsake father and mother, wife and child, to be saved? But the Scripture says plainly that they returned and did exactly the same work as before. They did not despise their service, but took it up again where they left off with all fidelity and I tell you that no bishop on earth ever had so fine a crook as those shepherds. (Roland H. Bainton, *The Martin Luther Christmas Book* [Philadelphia: Muhlenberg Press, 1948], p. 50)

First Sunday After Christmas

Old Testament Texts

The Old Testament lesson for the First Sunday After Christmas explores the implications of what it means when we confess that God is actually with us in this world. Isaiah 63:7-9 states how God is able to suffer with us, while Psalm 111 is an extended celebration of this fact.

The Lesson: *Isaiah 63:7-9*

A Savior for Hard Times

Setting. The lectionary has isolated the opening verses of a more extended community lament that probably included Isaiah 63:7–64:12. The larger context underscores how the recalling of God's graciousness and mercy in the opening verses is taking place at a time of need when the mercy of God is not readily apparent. Note how this larger lament recalls Israel's rebellion against God in Isaiah 63:10 and appeals for help in verse 15. The unit ends at Isaiah 64:12 without an immediate answer to the appeal for help, when the prophet asks God, "Will you keep silent, and punish us so severely?" The larger context is important for interpreting Isaiah 63:7-9, for it provides guidelines about how we affirm the presence of God that is central to Christmas, even at those times when we do not experience it. The text raises the questions, Is Christmas reliable? Do we have a savior for hard times?

Structure. We have seen how important the larger context of Isaiah 63:7–64:12 is for interpreting Isaiah 63:7-9. The internal structure of these verses also requires our attention. The unit separates into three parts. First, in v. 7 the prophet states that he will recount (literally, "bring to memory") God's character, especially those qualities of God that were evident in past actions. Thus the prophet recalls how God embodies the three qualities of goodness, mercy, and loving-kindness. Second, in v. 8a prophetic speech gives way to quotation of past divine speech: "For he [God] said, 'Surely they are my people, children who will not deal falsely.' " The quotation emphasizes how God is not worshiped in the abstract, but how the divine qualities of goodness, mercy, and lovingkindness are directed toward the people of God. Third, in vv. 8b-9 the prophet again speaks (note how God is once again referred to with the third person *he*) to interpret the divine quotation by providing illustration from the past of how God's qualities are directed toward Israel and how God is indeed present with the people of God.

Significance. The point of emphasis in Isaiah 63:7-9 is in the third section, when the prophet describes how God became Israel's savior. The prophet makes three points in this section. First and foremost—even during times of lament, when the salvation of God does not appear to be present—God is working as savior by suffering with us. Thus the prophet states in vv. 8b-9a: "He became their savior in all their distress." The second point that the prophet makes is to underscore just how intimately God has been with Israel in past afflictions. The next two lines in v. 9a read: "It was no messenger or angel but his presence that saved them." Because God had been so intimately present with Israel to the point of suffering with them, the third conclusion of the prophet is that God has been a reliable savior. Verse 9b reads: "In his love and in his pity he redeemed them; he lifted them up and carried them all the days of old." Here the prophet piles up verbs of salvation that spring from the love of God: God is able to redeem, to lift up, and to carry Israel.

Isaiah 63:7-9 is a powerful text for Christmas, for it is an unwavering affirmation of divine presence and salvation at all times but especially at times of lament, for at these times the savior is so intimate that God suffers with us. This reality allows the prophet to continue his lament through Isaiah 64:12.

The Response: *Psalm 148*

Celebrating the Reliability of God

Setting. Psalm 148 is probably best categorized as a hymn of praise in which imperative forms of the verb predominate (note the repetition of the imperative, "Praise" or "Let them praise!" in vv. 1, 2, 3, 4, 5, 7, 13, 14). The scope of the psalm is so wide in its call to praise that all aspects of creation are included. This large vision gives rise to a second characteristic of this hymn, which is the strong presence of wisdom motifs, especially evident in the listing of the natural order as those called upon to praise God.

Structure. The psalm separates into two parts, vv. 1-6 and 7-14. Verses 1-6 are a call to praise God from heaven, while vv. 7-14 repeat the command but this time from the earth. Each of these sections further separates into three parts: (1) Each section begins with a command to praise (from heaven, vv. 1-4 and from earth, vv. 7-12). (2) The command is followed in each case with a summary statement, which includes a reason why God should be praised (vv. 5 and 13). This section is signaled in each case through the repetition of the phrase "Let them praise the name of the LORD" (vv. 5*a*, 13*a*). The reason for praise from the hosts of heaven is that God created them (v. 5*b*), while earthly creatures must praise God because only the Lord is exalted on earth (v. 13*b*). (3) Finally, each section ends with a summary statement about God (vv. 6 and 14) in relationship to the hosts of heaven and earth (specifically Israel).

Significance. Psalm 148 provides a strong point of contrast to the lament that characterizes the Old Testament lesson. Over against the conclusion of Isaiah 63:7-9 that God is present in suffering, Psalm 148 turns all of creation (both heaven and earth) into an orchestra, whose music is meant to praise God, who is clearly present in every corner of the created order. This exuberant symphony of praise is at the very least jarring and potentially out of place when read as a response to Isaiah 63:7-9. In view of this potential problem, perhaps the best way to use Psalm 148 is to read the psalm backwards from the final verse. Verse 14 can be interpreted in the following manner. God is the subject of the verb *to exalt* or *to lift up* (Hebrew, *rum*), and furthermore, the psalmist tells us that God lifts up two things: a horn and praise. The indirect objects of God's activity consist of three different descriptions of Israel, each of which begins with the preposition *for*: *for* his people, *for* all his faithful, and *for* the people of Israel who are close to him. The syntax of the verse underscores two points: (1) It is God who generates praise for the people of God, and not the reverse, namely that the people of God generate praise for God; and (2) one reason why God is able to generate praise in the people of God is because God stays close to Israel. The spatial metaphor of God being close to the people of God is the point of connection between Psalm 148 and Isaiah 63:7-9. One text explores this confession of nearness at times of lament, while the other explores it during a time of praising. Each text, however, comes to the same conclusion: It is God who enables us both to lament and to praise. We do neither alone, because God is present in both situations.

New Testament Texts

There are no overt thematic connections between the two New Testament lessons for this Sunday, though each text focuses on the humanity of Jesus Christ, and each uses scripture to meditate on his sufferings in its own way. In Hebrews Jesus identifies fully with humankind in order to blaze the path of salvation living, which is completely in harmony with the testimony of the Old Testament; and in Matthew Jesus relives (with corrections) the story of Israel and brings God's will, as known through scripture, to fulfillment and moves it into the future.

The Epistle: *Hebrews 2:10-18*

Jesus, God's Human for the Salvation of Humankind

Setting. Although Hebrews opens like a treatise, it proceeds like a sermon and closes like a letter. The whole of Hebrews is an elaborate discourse on the superiority of Jesus Christ and the meaning of holding a Christian faith—all in the tone of a grand exhortation designed to encourage more than flaccid faith and life. The verses for this Sunday are from the sermonic proceedings of the writing.

Structure. Statements about Jesus in Hebrews 2:9—referring to his humanity, his suffering, and his vicarious death—are a preface to the lectionary reading. The prescribed verses (10-18) are a complex reflection upon the necessity of both Jesus' humanity and suffering for the salvation of humankind.

Verses 10-11 take up the idea of Jesus' and humanity's common human condition—which is the basis of his suffering's attaining our salvation. The reasoning of this passage begins with God and moves from Jesus to humanity. Then, vv. 12-13 establish this line of thought by offering an argument from scriptures. Finally, vv. 14-18 reverse the logic of vv. 10-11 and begin with the human condition and move to Jesus who accomplished the liberating (for humanity) destruction of the power of death (namely, "the devil") in his suffering, which forms an "expiation for the sins of the people."

Significance. "God works in mysterious ways" is a cliché, practically worn out from application to trivialities, but this passage, which deals with anything but a trivial matter (the salvation of humanity through God's work in Jesus), evokes that thought from many who read it. The author of Hebrews accounts for the humanity and suffering of Jesus by saying that it was "fitting" that God saved humanity through Jesus' sufferings because Jesus and humankind "have all one origin"— namely, our mutual humanity. Verses 10-11 demand two observations: (1) Given the whole of Hebrews, these verses are not minimizing Jesus' divinity in order to declare his humanity. Rather, they take seriously the real humanity of Jesus and the reality of his suffering that achieved salvation. Perhaps these emphases are a corrective to a docetic tendency that would minimize Jesus' humanity and ignore his suffering in order to focus on his divinity and his glory and their meaning for believers. (2) In saying that "it was fitting" that Jesus shared a common humanity with those whom he suffered to save, the author is recognizing that God might have worked otherwise, but God chose to work with and through reality rather than magic to achieve real results.

With the points of common humanity and salvation established, the passage assembles a set of Old Testament texts that form a kind of commentary on the ideas. At a glance the texts seem to be prooftexts, but they are much more; they explain something of the mysterious ways of God's salvation. By being human, Jesus was able to stand among humans and communicate with them (2:12, quoting Psalm 22:22), to do, in their midst, what they had not been able to do (2:13*a*, quoting Isaiah 8:17—see also II Samuel 22:3 and Isaiah 12:2), and through this work to assemble God's people as God worked through him (2:13*b*, quoting Isaiah 8:18).

The next five verses elaborate the argument further. The identification of Jesus, even in death, with humanity had the purpose of destroying the power of death in order to liberate those once in bondage because of their fear of death. Notice, there is liberation in freedom from the fear of death, not in being given immortality. When Jesus died and rose, he exposed the limits of the power of death and showed that God was the one who had final authority. God worked in Jesus to give humans real hope, not to make them something other than truly human. This is remarkable, for our passage began by describing God as "he for whom and by whom all things exist." Apparently humans suffered a loss of confidence in God when they stared death squarely in the face, but in Jesus the truth is shown—God can and does defeat the power of death. The creator is one worthy of the full trust and allegiance of humankind.

This is a strange theme for the Christmas season, but indeed as we celebrate the message of Christmas in preaching and worship—often with an emphasis on incarnation—it is good to know that at the heart of Jesus' birth is the saving grace of God at work to deal with the human condition, which has lapsed through fear into sin. Jesus confronts that sin as he defeats the power of death with the reality of his life, his suffering, and God's raising him from the dead. Thus our passage talks of *expiation*, which is atonement of sin; it does not refer to *propitiation*, the appeasing of a wrathful God, for the problem lies with humanity and the solution lies with God.

The Gospel: *Matthew 2:13-23*

God Overcomes Opposition as Jesus Unites the Past and the Future

Setting. The prescribed verses follow the story of the visitation of the wise men from the East who came looking for "the king of the

Jews,'' because they had seen a star signifying his birth. After unsuccessfully seeking the child at the court of Herod, the wise men found Jesus with his mother, and they gave him the luxurious tokens of their respect. Then, they were warned in a dream not to inform Herod of the child's whereabouts, so they returned home without paying another call on Herod. Knowing he has been deceived, Herod orders "the slaughter of the innocents.'' Then, we read of the flight to Egypt by the holy family. This is the final incident in Matthew's birth account.

Structure. The previous lectionary attempted to present a unified narrative by dropping Matthew 2:16-18 from the reading for this Sunday. The decision was unfortunate, for the story shows, in heinous detail, the earliest form of human opposition to God's work in and through Jesus Christ, an opposition that persists throughout the course of the adult Jesus' ministry. In one way, the inclusion of vv. 16-18 breaks the flow of the story of the holy family, but this is Matthew's manner of relating the gospel.

The storyline in the lectionary text is clear: With Jesus on the scene, Herod plans to eliminate him, but God intervenes to check Herod and to protect Jesus. Thus the holy family goes to Egypt and remains there until Herod's death. With Herod off the scene, God directs the family back to Israel, but Joseph avoids returning to Judea where Herod's son Archelaus was in charge.

Inherent in the structure of the story is the prominent motif of Jesus' constantly fulfilling scripture in the course of his life. The slaying of the infants in Bethlehem, the flight to Egypt, and the subsequent return (especially to Nazareth) are interpreted in terms of this theological conviction.

Significance. Pondering this story can lead to troubling questions that the scripture simply does not attempt to answer: Why didn't God save all the children in Bethlehem? Why did Joseph avoid Judea because of Archelaus (a relatively inept fellow) and go to Galilee where another of Herod's sons, Herod Antipas, was tetrarch? But Matthew simply does not pursue these points in his account; so, the questions must go unanswered, although there are many things this rich passage does tell us.

Matthew tells us that when God is at work, the powers of this world often align themselves in opposition, as Herod did when he learned of the birth of Jesus. But God is faithful to his promises and purposes and can be counted on to act to bring divine plans to fruition, as in the warning of the angel to Joseph. Throughout history, we can see—with the eyes of faith—God's work, human opposition, and God's faithfulness despite the opposition.

Joseph's obedience became the occasion for the fulfillment of God's promises of old. We see this in Matthew's statement that scripture was fulfilled and in his quotation of Hosea 11:1. If we ponder Matthew's story at this point, we learn a valuable lesson. The quotation from Hosea is striking, for it functions in the context of the Old Testament as a retrospective declaration about God's leading the nation of Israel out of bondage in Egypt. Any reader of Hosea would grasp this point. The line in Hosea is a historically descriptive one; it is not a prophetic prediction. What does Matthew mean? Nothing more and nothing less than that all of God's dealings with Israel are summarized, consummated, embodied, and realized in Jesus Christ. In Jesus all of God's work and all of God's words are made perfect. Israel's past becomes truly real, as Jesus relives and perfects Israel's story. Matthew makes a profound christological claim with these words, and we the readers should not press him for exact parallels.

In a striking manner vv. 19-23 reiterate the same points. Again, God intervenes to direct his purposes to completion. Again, Joseph's obedience—although now with a bit of input from Joseph—produces the fulfillment of scripture. But now it is not clear what text Matthew had in mind. Many possibilities have been suggested, but none really fits the statement. Perhaps more important than determining which text Matthew had in mind (a seemingly impossible task) is to ask how Matthew comprehended the statement. At Matthew 4:15, we see that Matthew understood Nazareth to be in Galilee of the Gentiles, so that he may be interpreting this childhood movement of the holy family to Nazareth to be a prefigurement of the Messiahship of Jesus being extended to the Gentiles. Thus in the passage at hand, one sees the child Jesus reliving God's past dealings with Israel and then living out God's future dealings with the Gentiles.

Christmas 1: The Celebration

This Gospel lesson—with its images of Jesus, Mary, and Joseph as refugees in Egypt and finally making their home in Nazareth—was originally chosen for the Roman calendar because that communion observes the First Sunday After Christmas as the Feast of the Holy Family. It is the inclusion of the story of the massacre of the children by Herod that may present a challenge to preachers and worship planners, as well as to those who will be hearing the lesson read. Its presence will be difficult to ignore, so how it is used should be carefully considered.

The Old Testament lesson and epistle are each pertinent to the massacre and the image of the holy family as refugees because of their emphasis on God's presence in the midst of suffering, God's identification with the powerless. A display of pictures of children who are suffering from the ruthlessness of the powerful would not be inappropriate somewhere in the church today. At least the intercessions should remember abused and starving children around the world. An excellent hymn text in response to the Gospel is "In Bethlehem a Newborn Boy" (No. 246 in *The Hymnal 1982*, The Church Hymnal Corp.). The following collect from the Church of England's *Alternative Service Book* is also recommended:

> Heavenly Father,
>   whose children suffered at the hands of Herod,
>   though they had done no wrong:
>   give us grace neither to act cruelly
>   nor to stand indifferently by,
>   but to defend the weak from the tyranny of the
>   strong;
>   in the name of Jesus Christ who suffered for us,
>   but is alive and reigns with you and the Holy
>   Spirit,
>   one God, now and for ever.

Prayers for refugees should also be included in today's intercessions.

It may be helpful to the preacher to remember that the sanctoral cycle of the Western Church has from very early times celebrated

three important saints' days on the three days immediately after
Christmas Day. December 26 is the feast of St. Stephen (hence the
reference in "Good King Wenceslaus"), who is described as being a
martyr in both will and deed. December 27 is the feast of St. John,
who is described as being a martyr in will but not in deed. And
December 28 is the feast of the Holy Innocents, who were martyrs in
deed but not in will. All are equally acceptable to God in the sacrifice
that they have offered with Christ. The three days remind us of just
what a serious business it is to celebrate Christmas!

The fact that today's psalm is an acrostic in Hebrew (see exegesis)
provides an interesting exercise for children who wish to be involved
in the planning of worship. They can provide a paraphrase of the
psalm using the English alphabet for the starting letters of each line,
but omitting the vowels, because they are also absent in the Hebrew.
Obviously, this is a project that should be begun weeks in advance.

Second Sunday After Christmas

Old Testament Texts

The Old Testament texts for the Second Sunday After Christmas are a celebration of God's salvation. Jeremiah 31:7-14 proclaims a new salvation to a remnant that will survive Israel's exile from the land at the hands of the Babylonians, while Psalm 147:12-20 is a celebration of God's power to save Israel.

The Lesson: *Jeremiah 31:7-14*

Salvation as Radical Reversal

Setting. Jeremiah 31:7-14 consists of two distinct oracles. Jeremiah 31:7-9 is an oracle of salvation addressed to Israel, or more specifically to the remnant of Israel that is either in the process of or about to experience a new salvation. This oracle begins with a prophetic messenger formula ("Thus says the Lord . . ."), moves to a proclamation of praise ("Sing . . . raise, shout . . . proclaim . . ."), and then gives the reason for praise by describing a new exodus for the remnant from the far corners of the world. Jeremiah 31:10-14 is an oracle directed to the nations rather than Israel. In this oracle the prophet describes what life in the land will be like for the remnant when the new exodus is completed.

Although the two oracles probably functioned independently at one time, one is able to see why the compilers of the book of Jeremiah have juxtaposed them. Taken together they describe both a new salvation and a new quality of life that will result from God's new exodus. Furthermore, each oracle underscores how God's new exodus and the quality of life in the land are a surprising reversal of conditions in our world, to which we all too often become accustomed.

Structure. Jeremiah 31:7-14 occurs in a larger section of the book of Jeremiah that is called the Book of Consolation, which consists of Jeremiah 30–33. This section of the book of Jeremiah stands out because the oracles of salvation, especially in Jeremiah 30–31, contrast sharply with the themes of judgment that dominate the remaining forty-eight chapters of the book. The isolation of the rather small Book of Consolation is an important starting point for interpreting Jeremiah 31:7-14. In particular, the result of having Jeremiah's salvation oracles gathered into one small section of the book is that salvation appears to be a fragile hope that floats in a sea of judgment. At the very least, the larger context of the book of Jeremiah is underscoring how God's salvation is a surprising reversal of conditions that dominate this world.

Significance. Salvation as God's surprising reversal of our expectations goes to the heart of the two oracles in Jeremiah 31:7-14. The reversal in Jeremiah 31:7-9 concerns the characteristics of the remnant. The survivors of the exile will not be the strong, as we would expect. Rather, those who will follow God through a new exodus are the weak, and four groups are specifically listed for us: the blind, the lame, pregnant women, and even women in labor. These are the persons that we would probably eliminate as candidates for a risky trip through the desert. Not so in God's new salvation. And furthermore, the prophet tells us that they will make the journey without stumbling. The reason for their miraculous safety is that this remnant is the "first-born" of God's new family. The prophet's incorporation of this exodus motif (compare Exod. 4:22-23 where Israel is proclaimed to be God's "firstborn" while they are in slavery in Egypt) brings to light another dimension of the four groups listed as God's remnant. The movement from blind and lame to pregnancy and conception itself is a movement from weakness to birth. The surprising news of the prophet is that God's new salvation is able to empower even the weakest to new birth. Such news runs counter to our everyday notions of power and success; we are taught that the best strategy is to invest in our strongest products and terminate the weakest.

The reversal in vv. 10-14 concerns the quality of life for the people of God once they return to the land. This oracle contrasts in a number of ways with the preceding one. Imagery of Zion takes center stage over the exodus; metaphors for God change from father to shepherd; language describing the people of God shifts from the motif of conception as God's first-born to representations of communal life in a garden characterized by cultic celebration; and most important, I think, the second oracle is addressed to the nations and not to the remnant.

Jeremiah 31:10-14 is saying at least two things. First, in describing the quality of life in the land for the remnant, the oracle completes the reversal that was started in vv. 7-9. When the blind and lame reach the land and live in the aura of God's goodness, the prophet tells us that there will be no more languishing and whatever mourning or sorrow remains will be transformed into joy and gladness (vv. 12*b*-13). Second, in being directed to the nations, Jeremiah 31:10-14 functions more as a declaration by God to the power structures that dominate our world, rather than a call to celebrate as was the case in vv. 7-9. The declaration is that there is a new power unleashed in the world that the nations must be aware of, and that as shepherd, God is the guarantor that those who live in this power will be satisfied with goodness.

The Response: *Psalm 147:12-20*

Celebrating New Life in the Land

Setting. Psalm 147:12-20 is able to function quite well as an independent hymn of praise, even though it presently is combined with two other short hymns of praise (vv. 1-6 and vv. 7-11). Note how vv. 1, 7, 12 are separate calls to praise God. The controlling metaphor that provides the background for vv. 12-20 is Zion. In fact, the hymn literally talks about the construction of the gates to Jerusalem in v. 13. This reference has prompted scholars to speculate on whether this hymn first functioned in the post-exilic community during the rebuilding of the wall of Jerusalem by Nehemiah. Whatever its exact historical context may have been, the imagery of Zion in Psalm 147:12-20 corresponds well to the second oracle in Jeremiah 31:10-14, where the new life in the land was described and celebrated.

This hymn, therefore, could be interpreted as further commentary on that text.

Structure. Psalm 147:12-20 separates into three parts. Verse 12 is a call for Zion to praise God. Verses 13-20*a* provide reasons for praising God. Verse 20*b* closes the psalm with a concluding call to praise.

Significance. Some of the hymns of Zion in the psalter run the danger of becoming celebrations of the status quo. They lend themselves to a reading in which the social and political security experienced by the worshiper is almost divinized to the point where it becomes the content of what God's salvation is all about. A celebration of God's rule from such a starting point might be summarized in the following way, ''All is right with my life, therefore God rules.'' An interpretation of Psalm 147:12-20 in isolation from the rest of Psalm 147 runs the danger of such an interpretation.

A closer look at the reasons for praise in vv. 13-20*a* will illustrate how Psalm 147:12-20 is not simply a celebration of the status quo. Two themes predominate in vv. 13-20*a* in providing a reason for why God must be praised. First, the point of focus in vv. 13-14 is that God is praiseworthy because God has power over creation. A variety of motifs arise in this section. God's rule in Zion is worthy of praise because it makes life secure, it carries blessing, it brings about peace and abundance. If the psalm stopped here, this hymn of praise would be little more than a celebration of all the things in our lives that give us immediate security. Although the second section is also a celebration of divine power in the world, there is nevertheless a slight shift in focus in vv. 15-20*a*. The point of focus is not a celebration of creation itself, but a celebration of God's word, which runs swiftly through the world (v. 15). This word of God is less predicable than simply equating God's rule with our security, or with forms of power that are most evident to us. A more complex view of God's rule arises in vv. 16-19. Here we are told that God both makes the threatening snow and melts it with his word. In this section, the psalmist seems to be saying that we cannot equate God's rule simply with powers in nature that surround us (whether they threaten us or provide security), because there are times when God's word can run counter to our expectations—the word can melt snow. In view of this situation, the psalmist tells us in v. 19 that the only way ultimately to evaluate the rule of God in this process is through Torah. This conclusion is our link back to Jeremiah 31:7-14 with its emphasis on God's salvation as a reversal that goes against our expectations.

New Testament Texts

The New Testament lessons are held together by their common focus on the blessings received by believers in the working of God's grace through Jesus Christ. Thus both texts view Christian life from a christological perspective and speak of the benefits of Christ. Individually the texts have other concerns: Ephesians boldly praises God for the advantages bestowed on believers; John tells of the Incarnation of Jesus Christ and practically sings the Christian importance of his person and work.

The Epistle: *Ephesians 1:3-14*

Blessing God from Whom All Blessings Flow

Setting. Normally Pauline letters open with a greeting, as Ephesians does in 1:1-2, and then a prayerful thanksgiving follows prior to the beginning of the body of the letter. Ephesians, however, has a blessing of God for the blessings that Christians have received (similar to a Jewish *berakah*) in 1:3-14; and then, 1:15-23 is the usual thanksgiving prayer report.

Structure. The lectionary reading comprises the verses of the divine blessing. The reading has two large parts with several thoughts or themes in each part:

1. Blessed be God the Father of our Lord Jesus Christ

   • who blessed us in Christ
   • who chose us in Christ
   • who destined us for adoption through Jesus Christ.

And all of God's activity results in the praise of the glory of God's grace.

2. In Christ himself believers have
- redemption and forgiveness according to grace
- wisdom and insight according to his good pleasure
- an inheritance according to God's plan—of which the Holy Spirit is a pledge.

The structure of the thought and the themes registered in the blessing is suggestive for the construction of sermons and portions of worship.

Significance. "Bless God!" was a favorite expression of an earlier generation of North American Protestant ministers, especially those from rural regions. Perhaps this linguistic pattern was adopted from the Old Testament, but it is equally likely that this parlance was picked up from reading Ephesians.

"Bless God" is a daring doxology in praise of the works of God which are simply too good to be true. The focus and the context of the "blessing" (read "praise") are set in relation to Jesus Christ. God has worked in and through Jesus Christ who is now Lord of the Christian community in order to "bless" Christian believers. The phrases of Ephesians 1:3-6 form a brief, cumulative, explanatory litany of God's blessing: God's blessing is tantamount to God's choosing and God's destining believers in Christ for adoption.

Before considering the ideas of choosing and destining (Presbyterians should take heart from this passage!), it is well to consider the phrase *in Christ*, for Ephesians says it is in Christ that believers are chosen and destined for adoption. Small seas of ink have been spent spelling out the significance of "in Christ." Some interpreters take the phrase as a synonym for "in church," while others relate "in Christ" to a form of Christian mysticism. The plain sense of the phrase in Ephesians is spatial. To express this sense of "in Christ" we may paraphrase, "in the context of the new creation established by the powerful grace of God at work in the life, death, and resurrection of Jesus Christ."

The statements that God chose and destined us for adoption "in Christ" make clear that it is by God's work and grace that we are brought into God's family. These verses convey a remarkable message about God, about God's work in Christ, and only secondarily do they provide information about us. The point of this passage is that

God works graciously through Christ for our benefit. The author is not interested in defining who is chosen and why, or who is not chosen and why not. The lines are theological, not anthropological, because the good news celebrated here is about God. The gospel has meaning for us, but it is not about us. Therefore, we must be careful with this potent text!

Afterword: The lines from the thanksgiving of the letter that follow our reading (1:15-18) unpack something of the meaning of God's blessings for us. The prayer asks that God give the believers the gift of intimate comprehension of God. Such understanding is not knowledge that comes through human ingenuity or effort—such as knowledge that comes from studying a math textbook. Rather, Ephesians asks for the gift of God's self-disclosure, which would come as an ever deepening relationship between God and the believers. In relation to God, the life of believers is characterized by the joy of hope and an awareness of the richness of God's grace. Believers have a new attitude, but it is not the result of positive thinking. It comes purely as a gift from God, and it activates a new way of living.

The Gospel: *John 1:(1-9) 10-18*

The Word in the World

Setting. These opening verses of the Gospel according to John are often called the prologue to the Gospel, for they function as a kind of frontispiece to the writing. In quasi-poetic fashion these lines declare themes that give the readers of John a profoundly theological perspective on the story, the teachings, and the truth-claims that follow.

Structure. The prologue is formed, as is the rest of the Gospel, by a rich, complex combination of historical memory, poetic expression about the person and work of Jesus Christ, and narrative commentary. The alternation between styles of writing, points of view, and types of reflection should provide much inspiration for those designing either preaching or worship.

One may cluster and contemplate the statements in these verses in terms of point of view: poetic confession (1:1-5, 10-12*a*, 14, 16);

historical reporting about John the Baptist (1:6-7, 15); and narrative commentary—frequently with a confessional bent—(1:8-9, 12b-13, 17-18). Or, one may divide the passage in terms of poetic (1:1-5, 10-12a, 14, 16) or prose (1:6-9, 12b-13, 15, 17-18) style.

Significance. There is room in this brief space to treat only the highlights of the passage. It opens with words similar to the creation story in Genesis 1. The idea at the heart of these lines is that the Word was with God in heaven before creation. The act of creation through the Word-present-with-God is recalled and emphasized by the Word's role as sustainer, but then the text mentions darkness, a poetic allusion to the Fall, and alters the Word metaphor for Jesus Christ into the metaphor of Light, a poetic allusion to Christ's work as Redeemer.

Verses 6-9 interrupt the poetry and move the mind of the reader into the recent past world of Palestine, mentioning John the Baptist and his limited role as prophetic witness to the coming Light (perhaps articulating a polemic against followers of the Baptist who made Messianic claims about him). The Word comes into the world as a past event, and is rejected by "his own people" (perhaps a reference to non-Christian Jews, but since the Word made all humans, the phrase may be a broader reference).The lines speak finally about the Word's redeeming effect on the lives of believers.

Verses 12b-13 explain that the empowerment of believers to be God's children is the work of God alone. Verse 14 meditates on the Incarnation, the historical interaction of believers with the Word-made-flesh, and the believers' perception of the glory of "the Son" who was filled with God's eternal love. Verse 15 underlines the validity of the christological claims advanced in the passage by citing the testimony of John the Baptist. Then, v. 16 speaks of the believers' sharing in the love of the Word-become-flesh; this is a kind of poetic explanation of the existential dimensions of redemption.

Finally, v. 17 explains in historical terms the statement of v. 16, drawing a comparison of law and love, of Moses and Jesus Christ (not so much to denounce Moses as to emphasize the superiority of Jesus Christ), and verse 18 boldly declares that the Son of God, Jesus Christ, has revealed the unseen Father to humankind.

The heart of this magnificent passage is christological. Jesus Christ, the Son of God, is God's eternal Word. As such, he is Creator,

Redeemer, and Revealer. All his work is characterized by love. From this passage we can contemplate the work of Christ and come to comprehend that all God's dealings with humanity are motivated by God's love. God is love, as John's Gospel tells us. Life is given, sustained, and redeemed because of and through God's love. And how do we know it? Because the unseen God has been revealed in Jesus Christ. The Word came into the world as an act of divine love to incorporate humanity into the primary experience of God's love.

Christmas 2: The Celebration

If January 6 follows this Sunday on a weekday, the preacher may wish to address some of the themes of Epiphany today. The Old Testament lesson can provide occasion for discussing how the celebrations of the sacraments are epiphanies, Christ working in the midst of the Church. In v. 12, the grain and the wine can be given a Christian reference to the Eucharist, and the oil to the anointing of baptism. "The young of the flock and the herd" in a Christian context can refer to the assembly of believers itself, and so the congregation can be led to examine the ways in which they experience Christ in their midst, in one another, and as they go about Christ's mission in the world. Epiphany themes are also present in the epistle with its emphasis on receiving a spirit of revelation and "having the eyes of your hearts enlightened." The reference to the "inheritance in the saints" can lead one to examine how we keep the Epiphany updated through the ongoing communion of saints. The exegetical section has already discussed the divisions that could be used in examining some of the content of the epiphany. The Gospel lesson, John's prologue, is fitting on this last Sunday of Christmas, because it would be appropriate on Christmas Day itself, and because it represents the Eastern tradition of the Church, which gave us the Festival of Epiphany. In the beginning of the year, we hear that in the beginning was the Word, which "became flesh and dwelt among us." The preacher may well wish to emphasize that central, scandalous fact from v. 14 as an antidote to the kind of spirituality that refuses to see God at work in the physical and that distrusts all things material.

Although the psalms are intended to be acts of corporate worship in response to the Old Testament lesson rather than a "scripture lesson" on their own, there is no reason why they cannot serve as the text for the sermon from time to time. Today, in early January, with the psalm's talk of snow, frost, and hail, this might be one of those times, but not for those reasons. The passage deals with the Word of God, which is also the subject of the other lessons. Here the activity of the Word is divided into what classically has been called natural and revealed theology: God's self-revelation in nature (vv. 15-18) and on the stage of history in particular ways (vv. 19-20)—the word that speaks creation into being in Genesis 1 and that becomes flesh in Jesus Christ in the Epiphany, which is being celebrated in this Christmas event. Here is a challenge for the doctrinal preacher.

In order to draw together all the themes of Christmas/Epiphany on this last Sunday of the season, "Angels from the Realms of Glory" is a particularly fitting opening hymn.

The application of a New Year's theme to this Sunday will be discussed in the Year C cycle.

Baptism of the Lord
(First Sunday After Epiphany)

Old Testament Texts

The central focus of the First Sunday After Epiphany is the baptism of Jesus. Isaiah 42:1-9 provides commentary for interpreting the significance of the baptism of Jesus for Christians, while Psalm 29 is a hymn of praise that can be used liturgically to celebrate the event.

The Lesson: *Isaiah 42:1-9*

The Commissioning of the Servant

Setting. Isaiah 42:1-4 (and perhaps vv. 5-9) is often described as one of the Servant Songs in "Second Isaiah" (Isaiah 40–55). Four times the anonymous exilic prophet, "Second Isaiah," speaks about a Servant of the Lord, who plays an important role in a new eschatological age that is about to begin among the exiled people of Israel. The Servant Songs are found in Isaiah 42:1-4, 49:1-6, 50:4-11, and 52:13–53:12. When these texts are read in isolation from their surrounding context, they appear to form a coherent literary unit in which the biography of a religious personality is described. Two interpretations of the Servant Songs in current biblical scholarship are important for Christian preaching. First, they provide commentary on the ministry and passion of Jesus as being the end-time messiah. In the earliest Christian tradition, the Servant Songs were interpreted as prophetic commentaries on the life and death of Jesus. For example, see Acts 8:26-40, where Philip provides a christological interpretation of Isaiah 53:7-8 to the Ethiopian eunuch. As important as this line of interpretation is for the Church, this reading has encouraged a single meaning for the Servant Songs that has not allowed these texts to function as scripture in their own right within the continuing life of the Church. A second line of interpretation has sought to provide a counterbalance by underscoring the collective emphasis of the Servant Songs, which designate all of Israel rather than an individual. This interpretation allows the texts to function in the present community by requiring that the whole people of God take on the characteristics of the suffering servant. A Christian proclamation of the gospel requires both of these emphases.

Structure. There is some debate about whether Isaiah 42:1-9 is a single unit or two distinct prophetic oracles. Isaiah 42:1-4 is clearly one of the Servant Songs. Verse 1*a* begins by describing the servant as being God's chosen one, and this oracle continues through v. 4 in a description of the function and characteristics of the servant, to which we must return in the following section. Verses 5-9 are best interpreted as a separate oracle. Notice how it begins in v. 5 with a messenger formula ("Thus says God, the Lord . . .") and how a servant is not mentioned any place in the unit. Thus it appears that in Isaiah 42:1-9 we have two distinct oracles that have been brought together in the formation of the book, and this insight is important for interpretation.

Significance. An interpretation of Isaiah 42:1-9 must take into consideration the juxtaposition of two distinct texts. Verses 1-4 appear to be describing a personality, the servant of God, who is endowed with the divine spirit. Scholars debate whether this is a reference to the anonymous prophet, a royal figure from the house of David, or even the Persian ruler Cyrus, whose rise to power is given a messianic interpretation (Isaiah 45:1). We will not solve this debate here. What is clear from the text, however, is the purpose of the servant. Three times (in vv. 1*b*, 3*b*, 4*b*) the prophet uses the word *justice* to describe the activity of the servant; this justice is directed to the nations (v. 1*b*), will be part of the structure of the earth itself (v. 4*b*), and will be reliable (v. 3*b*). The characteristics of the servant, outlined through a series of negations, provide some guidelines of what the prophet means by justice. First, justice is not rooted in the public display of power. Verse 2 underscores how the servant will not cry out in the street. Second, justice is not taking judgment to its logical conclusion, but may in fact require nurturing of whatever good is left. Thus v. 3 describes how the servant will not break the bruised reed or put out a dimly burning wick. Third, justice requires a dogged pursuit of that which is good. Verse 4 states how the servant will not fail or be discouraged in pursuing the good.

Isaiah 42:5-9 separates into three parts. First, v. 5 begins with the strong statement about God as being the Creator of the world and all peoples. Second, vv. 6-7 narrow the scope from the whole world to a particular person or people, who God has called out and strengthened for the purpose of being a covenant people. The use of covenant in this text does not mean simply that this person or these people are in a special relationship with God, but that they share obligations that God has to creation. These obligations are spelled out in the next three lines: to bring light to the nations, to open the eyes of the blind, and to release captives from darkness. These motifs of liberation are probably best interpreted as both metaphorical and literal. Light is both a political liberation and a new eschatological order in the world. Third, vv. 8-9 return to the theme of creation in order to provide assurance for the vision that was spelled out in vv. 6-7.

The juxtaposition of Isaiah 42:5-9 with the description of the servant in vv. 1-4 creates some ambiguity. Is this oracle meant to be a continuation of vv. 1-4 and thus a further description of an individual, or is it addressed to all of Israel? The use of *you* in v. 6 is singular, which favors an interpretation of vv. 5-9 as being a continuation of the individual servant in vv. 1-4. The use of *a covenant people* at the end of v. 6 along with the plural *you* in v. 9 suggests that the whole community of Israel is being addressed in the second oracle. The point of the ambiguity is that both interpretations must be incorporated for a proper reading of the Servant Songs. The prophet saw God bringing about a new eschatological reality through a variety of individuals—a Davidic monarch, Cyrus, and even the prophet himself. For such a reality to take root required that Israel also embody the qualities of the servant. The same holds true for the Church today. We have reinterpreted the eschatological vision of "Second Isaiah" in the light of the passion of Jesus, but in doing this we are assuming the obligation of embodying the qualities of the servant. Thus we celebrate today the commissioning of both Jesus and ourselves as his Church.

The Response: *Psalm 29*

Celebrating the Power of God

Setting. Psalm 29 is a powerful hymn of praise. It celebrates the rule of God over nature through the motifs of a storm. The frequent repetition of "the voice of the Lord" (seven times in vv. 3-9) is best interpreted as thunder, which is accompanying a storm that has rolled off the Mediterranean Sea and is hitting the coast. From there it shakes the cedars of Lebanon in the north before it swings southward to cast bolts of lightning in the southern wilderness of Kadesh. The imagery is vivid and ancient. Scholars have traced many of these motifs to the Canaanite culture that preceded Israel and have even suggested that Psalm 29 was originally a psalm of Baal, the Canaanite God of rain, with YHWH now edited in.

Structure. Psalm 29 follows the structure of a hymn, and thus it separates into three parts: an introduction in vv. 1-2, which functions as a call to praise; an enumeration of the praiseworthy acts of God in vv. 3-9; and a conclusion in vv. 10-11, which gives reasons why God should be praised while also calling the worshiper to praise God. The hymn is tightly woven in its construction. For example, the introduction and conclusion balance each other with four lines, while each also refers to "the Lord" four times.

Significance. Psalm 29 is a celebration of divine power in this world, and as such it functions well as an extension of the second oracle in Isaiah 42:1-9, where the creative power of God was proclaimed to provide assurance to the servant community in vv. 5-9. Two themes in particular stand out as providing assurance to a servant people of God. First, Israel and her neighbors had a tendency to divinize the power of weather (the god, Baal) because of its importance in their everyday lives. Thus by taking on motifs from nature to celebrate the rule of God, the psalmist has actually entered into a polemic about the character of power in this world—namely, that what appears most powerful to us in our everyday lives (Baal) may not necessarily be the case. Without such revelation, the ideal of being a servant people would be ludicrous. Second, in view of the first conclusion, the psalmist encourages us to look for real power in this world in worship and not in our everyday lives. The introduction calls the community to worship (vv. 1-2) while the conclusion assures them of God's power in their midst (vv. 10-11). The introduction and conclusion provide the framework for interpreting the statement of faith about the power of God in the thunderstorm.

Psalm 29 challenges us to examine how Baal is still an active deity in our own lives. Baal may no longer be limited to the security of a thunderstorm in an agricultural society, but this does not mean that this god may not exist for us in a modern form of blue chip stocks or some other kind of investment property that gives us the illusion of security.

New Testament Texts

The texts for this Sunday are held together by common associations with two themes: (1) God's anointing of Jesus with the Holy Spirit and (2) baptism. In Matthew's Gospel these subjects are explicit, but in the Acts text, only the mention of Jesus' being anointed with the Spirit is overt. One relates the Acts test to baptism through the mention of the forgiveness of sins in Christ's name (Acts 10:34-43), which is a baptismal theme.

The Epistle: *Acts 10:34-43*

God's Impartial Salvation

Setting. We usually think of Paul as the apostle to the Gentiles, but these verses show us Peter (the so-called apostle to the Jews) going to and addressing Cornelius and his household. In the context of the mission to Israel, the Holy Spirit shatters the boundaries between Jews and Gentiles. In a brief moment of the story, we foresee the course of the gospel reaching humans in all nations.

Structure. There are three clear segments of the speech by Peter: First, vv. 34-35 declare Peter's newfound perception of the impartiality of God and of the universal acceptability of God-fearers to God. Second, vv. 36-42 offer christological teaching that is laced with and backed by allusions to Old Testament texts or ideas. Third, v. 43 states that the testimony of the prophets makes known that "everyone who believes in him receives forgiveness of sins through his name."

Significance. Within the broad structure of this passage, there are several crucial themes of which we shall consider four. First, Peter declares the impartiality of God. The literal sense of the text makes plain what this means, saying, "God is no face-receiver!" Outward appearances do not influence God, for God does not view persons according to human standards. Rather, we learn that God is interested in the attitude of humans toward God: what God wants is for persons to be reverentially respectful of God so that they do God's will. It is dangerous, however, to focus on this point apart from the broader currents of the Acts account, for it is easy to misconstrue this text into a justification of a "works righteousness." Notice, Cornelius was in prayer, but the vision he experienced came as an act of grace. The mention in 10:31 of the alms that Cornelius had given should tip us as to the meaning of the text. Almsgiving was the exercise of righteousness, the recognition of God's blessings. God blessed Cornelius, and Cornelius demonstrated his gratitude; Cornelius was not trying to buy God's favors, he was celebrating them! Such an attitude is the one God commends, and among those who have such a disposition, God knows no favorites.

Second, Peter declares that as Jesus was anointed with the Holy Spirit and did the work of God, he was the very demonstration of the power of God. It is this Jesus who is now Lord of all. When we humans have questions about God and God's will for our lives, to borrow the language of popular piety, Jesus is the answer. Want to know God? Look at Jesus. Want to know God's will for our lives? Recognize that Jesus is Lord and realize that his way of living is to be ours if he is Lord. Christian thought and life are not astrophysics;

not reserved for those with sufficient brain-power to figure out God. Remember, God is no face-receiver.

Third, in vv. 38-40 we see the crucial theme of God's initiative, action, and achievement (in Jesus Christ), which is met with human resistance, rebellion, and rejection (of Jesus Christ), which is overturned by divine affirmation, vindication, and exaltation (of Jesus Christ). This christologically focused pattern of divine-human interaction is the framework of our lives. At the outset is the news of God's love. But at the heart of the exchange is the reality of our sinfulness. Yet we do not have the last word, for God triumphs and grace abounds so that the message is gospel, not tragedy.

Fourth, vv. 42-43 declare that Christ commands his followers to witness to the work of God by telling others that God has authorized Jesus to be the judge of the living and the dead. The christological truth at the heart of such testimony is that God has made Jesus Christ larger than life. With such power at work, it is then understandable how everyone who believes in him (having heard the testimony of his followers) receives forgiveness of sins through his name. Because Christ is larger than life, human lives can and are transformed!

The Gospel: *Matthew 3:13-17*

Jesus: Fulfilling All Righteousness

Setting. This story not only follows but brings to a climax the preceding account of John the Baptist's preaching, person, practices, and prophecy. Matthew 3:1-12 focused on John, the man, his message, and his ministry, but 3:13-17 alters the focus as it builds on the story about John. We now meet ''the stronger one'' of whom John spoke.

Structure. There are three distinct movements in this account: (1) In v. 13, Jesus appears in the contest of John's ministry, following on the heels of the Baptist's prophecy about the one who was coming after him. (2) In narrative form, vv. 14-15 takes up the very real and even problematic question of why Jesus submitted to John's baptism of repentance. (3) The final verses (16-17) recount Jesus' vision of the opened heavens, the descent of the Spirit upon him, and the declaration of the voice of God. A sermon or elements of liturgy might either follow the broad movements of the text or simply focus on the profound christological elements of vv. 16-17.

Significance. Jesus comes in fulfillment of the prophecy of John the Baptist, but in Matthew's Gospel, Jesus is more than a one-time prophecy-fulfiller; rather, in Matthew's telling of the gospel, everything about Jesus—from his conception, through his ministry, to his cross and Resurrection—is a fulfillment of prophecy. Repeatedly in the Gospel there are instances of Jesus' fulfilling prophecy—often accompanied by a note from Matthew informing the reader that fulfillment had occurred. Because Matthew understands Jesus to be the Son of God, he portrays Jesus moving in fulfillment of prophecy in such a way that Jesus often redefines the meaning of God's promises and purposes in surprising ways. Here, for example, as Jesus realizes John's prediction of his coming in power and judgment, he does the unlikely: Jesus, the Son of God, submits himself to John for baptism—but a baptism of repentance! This first unlikely event in Matthew's story of the adult Jesus' ministry is a foretaste of the great absurdity to come—namely, that the Son of God will suffer and die an ignoble death on a cross in order to accomplish the salvation of humanity. These unlikely events occur, we learn, because Jesus lives doing the will of God, a will that is revealed in Jesus and declared in the gospel and that is grasped, not by logic, but by faith in the recognition of Jesus as the Son of God. Jesus lives fulfilling prophecy in unpredictable ways, because he lives doing and revealing God's righteousness!

As we read or hear Matthew's account, we are struck by the dramatic events of the opened heavens, the descent of the dove, by the grand words of God from heaven. This magnificent moment in Matthew's account gives both the private and public confirmations of the identity of Jesus as the Son of God. Remarkably Jesus' vision of the opened heavens and the descending dove seem, in Matthew's telling, to be Jesus' private perceptions: he is the one who sees. But the word from God is a public declaration. This framing of the events distinguishes Matthew's Gospel in comparison with the other New Testament versions of this story. Matthew displays a concern to relate the depth of Jesus' personal, even private, comprehensions; yet, the voice of God makes clear the meaning of Jesus' insights.

This story gives us Matthew's understanding of the person and work of Jesus Christ. Through this story we are told and given evidences of who Jesus is: the Son of God. Notice, however, that Matthew is not so much interested in the ontological dimensions of Jesus' divine Sonship; rather, he shows us a Jesus who is the dynamic Son of God, committed—beyond our abilities to reason—to doing the will of God. In and through this story, Matthew relates more than his personal perceptions about Jesus (although he certainly does this); indeed, Matthew tells us through God's public declaration at the outset of Jesus' ministry that Jesus is the Son of God, who is always ready and able to fulfill God's will.

Epiphany 1 (The Baptism of the Lord): The Celebration

The celebration of Jesus' baptism on the First Sunday After Epiphany is patterned after the practice of the Eastern church and reminds us that it is his baptism that inaugurates his ministry in all the Gospels. This event calls us at the beginning of the year to remember our baptisms and examine again how faithful we have been to our call to follow Christ. The renewal of baptismal vows can be significant following a sermon that has dealt with the relationship between baptism and the work of ministry. Both sermon and liturgy should emphasize that the ministry under discussion is Christ's ministry, not ours or even the Church's, lest the enterprise degenerate into a celebration of our own good intentions and an orgy of goal setting.

Peter Chrysologus, a great preacher of the fifth century, spoke of today's celebration in this way:

Today, as the psalmist prophesied, "The voice of the Lord is heard above the waters." What does the voice say? "This is my beloved Son, in whom I am well pleased."

107

Today the Holy Spirit hovers over the waters in the likeness of a dove. A dove announced to Noah that the flood had disappeared from the earth; so now a dove is to reveal that the world's shipwreck is at an end for ever. (*Christian Prayer: The Liturgy of the Hours* [Baltimore: Helicon Press, 1976], p. 1760.)

Those lines quoting today's lections might be used as a heading or part of the cover for the bulletin on this day.

Today's Gospel portrays baptism as a Trinitarian activity. The Son who receives the Spirit's anointing is testified to by the Father. This anointing should at least remind enthusiastic Christians that one should not speak of "baptism of the Spirit" with no reference to or acknowledgment of the other divine Persons.

The color for today continues to be white or gold. "Hail to the Lord's Anointed" is an appropriate hymn for this day because of its emphasis on Jesus' ministry. The renewed emphasis on the Baptism of the Lord as a special day in the Church's calendar has produced several new hymns in many new denominational hymnals. Among these are:

"Anointed of God, How Can We See You" (United Church of Christ)
"Christ, When for Us You Were Baptised" (Episcopal Presbyterian)
"I Come, the Great Redeemer Cries" (Episcopal)
"Lord, When You Came to Jordan" (Presbyterian)
"The Sinless One to Jordan Came" (Episcopal)
"When Jesus Came to Jordan" (Presbyterian, United Methodist)
"When Jesus Went to Jordan's Stream" (Episcopal) Another translation is "To Jordan Came the Christ, Our Lord" (Lutheran).

The World Council of Churches publication *With All God's People: The New Ecumenical Prayer Cycle—Orders of Service* has a special service for the affirmation of baptism that can be easily adapted for use on this day in a local congregation (write to World Council of Churches, 475 Riverside Drive, Room 915, New York, NY, 10115-0050).

Liturgical presiders who are doing both baptisms and a reaffirmation of baptism should think carefully about the amount of water used in each event. If the people are sprinkled at the reaffirmation, then much more water should be used for the actual baptisms in order to have the signs clearly distinguished and not give the impression that the reaffirmation is some kind of rebaptism. Where immersions are not possible for baptisms, then a generous pouring should be employed. If at all possible, arrange the setting for the baptism so that the water can be seen and heard by as many as possible.

Second Sunday After Epiphany

Old Testament Texts

As the Gospel lesson for this week indicates, the baptism of Jesus remains the point of focus, and thus the theme of commissioning continues to play a central role in this Second Sunday After Epiphany. The continuity of theme in the Gospels is also carried through in the Old Testament lessons, because Isaiah 49:1-7 is the second of the Servant Songs. Both Isaiah 49:1-7 and Psalm 40:1-11 explore what it means to be commissioned as the people of God. Isaiah 49:1-7 outlines the character and quality of our mission in this world, while Psalm 40:1-11 provides guidelines for what our responsibilities are in worship.

The Lesson: *Isaiah 49:1-7*

The Hiddenness of God's Salvation

Setting. In the discussion of the Old Testament lessons for the First Sunday After Epiphany, we noted that there were four Servant Songs (Isaiah 42:1-4; 49:1-6; 50:4-11; 52:13–53:12) and that they provide a continuous biography of the servant even though they are presently separated in the book of Isaiah. Isaiah 42:1-4 was a divine proclamation about the role of the servant to bring about justice in the larger world. This proclamation of a universal justice that emanates from God and is channeled through the servant provides important background for our interpretation of Isaiah 49:1-7.

Structure. There are a number of problems in structuring Isaiah 49:1-7. The first problem is whether the second Servant Song includes v. 7. Most scholars would say that it does not. Note, for example, how there is a full introductory formula in v. 7 ("Thus says the Lord . . ."), which marks this verse off from vv. 1-6. Thus we should note that the lectionary reading consists of two distinct texts, in much the same way as Isaiah 42:1-9 did last week. The juxtaposition of two texts in one lectionary reading prompts us to raise the question of how the oracle in v. 7 functions in relation to the Servant Song in vv. 1-6. The second problem concerns some of the language and internal structure of the Servant Song itself. A comparison of v. 2 (the call of the servant already from the womb) and vv. 5-6 (the mission of the servant to Israel) to v. 3 (the apparent identification of the servant with Israel) underscores once again the ambiguity of whether the servant is an individual or post-exilic Israel (see the discussion in Year A, First Sunday After Epiphany). The ambiguity is probably intentional and thus should not be eliminated. Yet the indicators in Isaiah 49:1-6 favor an interpretation of the servant as an individual who can stand over against the people of God. It is this point of interpretation that gives rise to the following three-part outline:

1. The opening address and commissioning of the servant (vv. 1-2)
2. Three divine speeches to the servant (vv. 3-6)
3. A concluding oracle of salvation for the nations (v. 7)

Significance. The central question in preaching Isaiah 49:1-7 is this: Who embodies the servant qualities that are necessary for revealing the hiddenness of God's salvation? Verses 1-2 present the opening address and the commission of the servant. As in Isaiah 42:1-4, the nations are being addressed; it is the coastlands and the people from afar that must pay attention to the following message. The commissioning of the servant in v. 2 underscores two things: first, that the servant is commissioned to speak for God; and second, that the message of the servant is a new word for the nations, or to use the imagery of the text, the words, which will be "like a sharp sword" or like a "polished arrow," have been "hidden away" by God until now.

Although vv. 3-6 complete the Servant Song, in the context of the lectionary reading they compose the second section. This section consists of a dialogue between God and the servant in the following format: divine speech (v. 3), response by the servant (v. 4), divine speech (v. 5*a*), response by the servant (v. 5*b*), and divine speech (v. 6).

The first divine speech in v. 3 addresses the servant in the first line ("You are my servant.") and then appears to identify the servant with Israel in the second line ("Israel, in whom I will be glorified."). Commentators differ on how to interpret the second line. It may be a later gloss or addition that has been added to the text in order to identify the servant with the post-exilic community. Another interpretation suggests that the second line is not synonymous with the first (that it is not an identification of the servant and Israel) but that Israel is the object of the servant's commission. This latter interpretation fits well with the thematic development of the following dialogue. The servant's response to this commission is that it has not been successful and that consequently he has "labored in vain." The response suggests that there is tension between the servant and the larger community of the people of God.

The second divine speech in v. 5*a* reaffirms the call of the servant to Israel. Once again there are problems of interpretation in the divine speech. The NRSV translation of the task of the servant reads, "to bring Jacob back to him [God], and that Israel might be gathered to him [God]." This translation follows the marginal notes in the Hebrew Bible (the Masoretic text). The text itself says something different: "to bring Jacob back to him, but Israel was not gathered in." Most commentators and translations follow the marginal notes for translation and interpretation so that both lines say the same thing, but they need not. Furthermore, the text of the Hebrew Bible, as we presently have it, prepares the reader better for the third divine speech.

After the servant's response in v. 5*b* that his strength rests only in God (note the third-person references to God in these lines), the divine reply is that the servant's commission will be expanded beyond the boundaries of Israel to all the nations, so that God's salvation reaches to the ends of the earth. This concluding speech of God is the "hidden" word in vv. 1-2 that the servant wished to address to the nations.

The divine oracle in v. 7 must be interpreted as an expansion of the third speech of God in v. 6, and as such it is the point of focus for the Old Testament lesson. Several things are noteworthy about this verse when it is read in conjunction with the Servant Song in vv. 1-6. First, the emphasis is universal, as was the case in the Servant Song. The nations (kings and princes) will see something that they had previously been blinded to, which will prompt them to worship. Second, what the nations will see is a surprising reversal with regard to strength—namely, that God chooses weakness (the despised, abhorrent, and servant) as a channel for power. This reversal is the light to the nations that the servant embodies in his character. Third, v. 7 reintroduces ambiguity concerning the identity of the servant, for God is identified as the "Redeemer of Israel." The ambiguity leaves us with a question, and perhaps that is the point of the text. Do we, as the people of God, embody the qualities of the servant, or must God look elsewhere to find a light for the nations? The dialogue between God and the servant about the post-exilic people of God in vv. 3-6 is an ongoing conversation that now includes ourselves.

The Response: *Psalm 40:1-11*

The Gift of Thanksgiving

Setting. Psalm 40:1-11 is classified as a Song of Thanksgiving from an individual. It is really the first part of Psalm 40, which concludes with the Psalm of Lament in vv. 12-17. Most scholars agree that vv. 1-11 and vv. 12-17 are distinct psalms that have been brought together in their present context, with the result that the Song of Thanksgiving (vv. 1-11) about a past salvation of God provides the psalmist with confidence to ask God for still further help in the Psalm of Lament (vv. 12-17).

Structure. Psalm 40:1-11 separates into three parts. In vv. 1-3a the psalmist recounts God's help in a past situation of need. Verses 3b-8 shift the focus to the present worshiping community in order to explore the effect of God's past help to the psalmist on this larger community. In vv. 9-11 the faithfulness of the psalmist in giving thanks to God in worship is stated in vv. 9-10 as a basis for a request for further divine mercy (v. 11).

Significance. Psalm 40:1-11 explores one aspect of what it means to be commissioned that we frequently overlook—namely, that we are called to give thanks to God in the setting of worship. The motif of thanksgiving is introduced in v. 3*a*. The striking feature of this verse is that thanksgiving is itself a gift that God gives. It is God who put a new song of praise in the mouth of the psalmist. The result of thanksgiving as being God's gift rather than something that originates with the worshiper is that it must be shared with the larger worshiping community. The second section of the psalm describes how the psalmist acts out liturgically this commission to give thanks in worship. Finally, the psalm ends in vv. 9-11 with the psalmist recounting how the commission to give praise for past salvation has been fulfilled "in the great congregation."

New Testament Texts

With these texts the lectionary moves into ordinary time. The lesson from I Corinthians begins a sequential reading of selected texts from that epistle that will continue up to the Last Sunday After Epiphany (Transfiguration Sunday). The Gospel text from John interrupts the otherwise sequential series of readings from Matthew that occurs through the Sundays after the Epiphany; it is inserted into the Matthean sequence as a follow-up to the lesson from last Sunday. Whereas the baptism account in Matthew essentially gave us Jesus' point of view on the events, this text from John offers the Baptist's testimony to the events and his interpretation of the person of Jesus Christ.

The Epistle: *I Corinthians 1:1-9*

The Radical Reformation of Life

Setting. These opening verses of I Corinthians form the salutation and the thanksgiving of Paul's letter. Paul names Sosthenes, a former resident of Corinth (see Acts 18:1-18, especially verse 17), as the coauthor of the epistle, and throughout this letter, Paul shows that he has good information about the situation in Corinth. In general, the situation is this: Some of the members of the church in Corinth are quarreling and forming competitive cliques, each of which claims to be more spiritual than the others. In short, spiritual arrogance is tearing apart the Body of Christ, as one group after another struts its spiritual superiority. Paul writes to address this multifaceted mess, which at core amounts to one thing: boasting.

Structure. There are two distinct parts to this text. First, vv. 1-3 form the salutation of the letter, and there are three subsections to this greeting. (A) Paul names himself and Sosthenes as the authors of the letter; (B) the Corinthian believers are addressed as a group as the recipients of the epistle; and (C) the salutation concludes with a greeting of "grace and peace" from God and Christ. Second, vv. 4-9 offer an epistolary thanksgiving.

Significance. The wording of the seemingly benign opening of this epistle connotes the radical reframing and reorganization of life's relationships through the work of God in Jesus Christ. Paul says he was called by God's will to be sent by Jesus Christ (*apostle* means "one who is sent"). That is, he is not a self-determined individual; rather, his life is dominated and directed by God. Furthermore, the manner in which Paul refers to himself and to others in this address is evidence that God's will had radically reformed their lives. Paul thinks of himself in terms of the will of God, and he names others in ways that show that God had grasped their lives. Sosthenes is called Paul's brother, not because of any human bond, but because they have been united in Christ in a fraternal bond as children of God. This redefinition is remarkable, for from Acts we learn that Sosthenes was the former leader of the Corinthian synagogue who filed charges against Paul with the proconsul Gallio. Practical human opposition was obliterated through radical divine reconciliation. Moreover, Paul calls the collection of believers in Corinth "the church of God in Corinth." Another way to say this would be "God's assembly in Corinth," which makes it clear that the church exists in, through, and because of God's work among them and in their lives. Thus the believers are identified in terms of their relationship to God.

The wording of Paul's salutation also tells us that as Christians we do not go it alone. Paul is no "Lone Ranger for Jesus." He works on the mission field in relation to Sosthenes and many other fellow workers (Barnabas, Timothy, Titus, Prisca, Aquila, and others).

Indeed, Paul does not even think about the congregation in Corinth in isolation from the worldwide community of those whose lives have been transformed and redefined in God's work through Jesus Christ; as he calls the Corinthians "the church of God," he thinks of them in relation to "all those who in every place call on the name of our Lord Jesus Christ, both their Lord and ours." Clearly Christian identity is formed, not by looking to or at ourselves, but in our God-willed relationship to our universal Lord, Jesus Christ.

The greeting punctuating the salutation (v. 3) shows the degree to which Christian life and living have been radically reformed through Christ. Paul (and Sosthenes) declares "grace and peace," not mere "greetings" to the Corinthian Christians. It is the difference between meeting the monarch of England and greeting her with "God save the Queen!" rather than "Hi." Grace is the work of God for the salvation of humankind, and peace is the result of God's labor in Jesus Christ.

Finally, in the thanksgiving (vv. 4-9) Paul signals the cause of his joy and his concern for the Corinthians. God richly blessed these believers with "spiritual gifts," a topic of major concern in the body of this letter, but the Corinthians have misunderstood and abused God's blessings—as Christians too often do. Forgetting that God is the common source of whatever "spiritual gifts" they possess, the Corinthians behave as if they themselves were to be credited with their Christian capacities. Paul subtly reminds them that God granted them all that they have and are in Christ and that they are called to steadfastness in Christ (not dissension), for God who is faithful sustains them (and us) as they (and we) live, awaiting the day of our Lord Jesus Christ. Too often we "get ahead" of ourselves and forget that God's good gifts are given to sustain us in mutual love; they are not private matters that elevate us over one another.

The Gospel: *John 1:29-42*

Serving God and Knowing Jesus Christ—the Purpose of Our Lives

Setting. Following the prologue to the Gospel (vv. 1-18), verses 19-34 are a two-part testimony from John the Baptist. First, the

Baptist testifies before the representatives of the priests and Levites in vv. 19-28, an essentially negative passage where John denies any messianic identity for himself and minimizes his own importance in comparison to the one coming after him. Then, in vv. 29-34, John sees Jesus and gives a positive witness that confirms Jesus' identity as the Spirit-anointed, elect Lamb of God who takes away the sin of the world. The final verses of the lesson (35-42) tell of the call of the first disciples. Either vv. 29-34 or 35-42 are suitable for preaching. In what follows, we shall focus on the first set of verses.

Structure. The structure of this passage exists in the spiraling logic of John the Baptist's testimony. In v. 29 John sees Jesus and testifies concerning who he is (the Lamb of God) and what he does (takes away the sin of the world); and v. 30 complements these words about Jesus' person and work, giving John's declaration that Jesus is the one coming after him—though John's testimony also refers to Jesus' "preexistence"! Together vv. 29-30 form a crescendo of christological confession. Then, in v. 31 the Baptist offers a slight qualification: he did not know Jesus, but John's ministry of baptism was wholly in preparation for Jesus' appearance. Next, vv. 32-33 look back to the baptism of Jesus and give John's testimony in confirmation of the descent of the dove on Jesus. John declares that this was a God-given sign that he might know the unknown one for whom he labored. Finally, in v. 34 John briefly reiterates his witness, in part confirming his identification of Jesus, but now speaking of Jesus as the elect of God, still another christological confession.

Significance. Although John the Baptist did not know Jesus, he was given a commission by God to work in a ministry that was preparatory for the appearance of Jesus. Not only was John given a commission, apparently he was given a promise that God would make the one who was coming after him known to him in God's own good time. And so, John had worked; and, in turn, God had made good on the promise, for Jesus had indeed appeared and God had shown John who he was in a most dramatic way. As John recognized Jesus, he was able to speak about him in a variety of ways, declaring who Jesus was and what he had come to do. Remarkably John served God faithfully in behalf of Jesus, although he did not know who Jesus was; the Baptist had ministered in faith and hope.

Today God calls us, as God called John the Baptist, to service in faith and hope. But, as Christians we have a certitude in our service that is greater than that initially given to John. We do not labor in the hope of one day meeting a now-unknown messiah, for Jesus Christ has already come. Because God has already revealed Jesus Christ, our service to God is somewhat different from John's. John moved among humans declaring God's ways, calling for repentance, and promising that one day God would act in power in the person of one who was coming. But, notice that when Jesus appeared on the scene, John's focus shifted from the future to the present.

If we are true to God's calling, we too focus on the reality of God's work in Jesus Christ. So, we look back at God's past, then forward to the present, and on to God's future, and we see and confess that in Jesus Christ God has unified the times so that salvation is real. Our hope is beyond us in God's future, yet that future has already been made real, so that our faith takes on the liberating dimensions of our hope as a current reality through faith in Jesus Christ. As we serve God, we know Jesus Christ as real, and as we know Jesus Christ, we serve God in a faith that appropriates the power of God-given hope. By bringing God's future into the past and present, Jesus Christ confronts the sin of the world with the power of God, and so, Jesus takes away sin as he manifests the life of God, which itself overcomes sin in Jesus own life, death, Resurrection, and gift of the Spirit.

Epiphany 2: The Celebration

John the Baptist's proclamation at the beginning of today's gospel is the source for the liturgical hymn *Agnus Dei* (O Lamb of God), which is used in many services just prior to the receiving of communion. Its traditional form is as follows:

> O Lamb of God, that takest away the sins of the world,
>   have mercy upon us.
> O Lamb of God, that takest away the sins of the world,
>   have mercy upon us.
> O Lamb of God, that takest away the sins of the world,
>   grant us thy peace.

Another version is:

> Jesus, Lamb of God, have mercy on us.
> Jesus, bearer of our sins, have mercy on us.
> Jesus, redeemer of the world, give us your peace.

Its appearance in the gospel today makes its liturgical use particularly appropriate. If the Eucharist is not celebrated, it may still be used as an introduction to the Peace, since the last line is "grant us your peace." This also emphasizes that it is *Christ's* peace we are sharing rather than our own satisfaction with being in each other's company. In a non-eucharistic liturgy, it may be said or sung following the confession of sin before the words of assurance or absolution. The Peace would then complete that part of the liturgy, as follows:

Prayer of Confession
The Agnus Dei (said or sung, responsively or in unison)
Words of Assurance (or Absolution)
The Peace (introduced with the greeting,
  "The Peace of the Lord be always with you."
  "And also with you.")

Although John is not read consecutively through the year, the preacher should be aware that this image of Jesus as the Lamb of God at the beginning of ordinary time will be picked up again on Good Friday when John's passion narrative is read. There the Crucifixion occurs on the Day of Preparation, the day when the lambs were slaughtered for the Passover. Last Sunday the emphasis was on commissioning to ministry; today there is an implied identification of baptism with suffering and death as a part of that ministry. This can provide an opportunity to explore further the implication of our baptism as a dying both to and for the world. The epistle provides an opening to discuss baptism as the avenue to sanctification and to explain "saints" as the company of the baptized who have been the recipients of the grace of a faithful God. Martin Luther King, Jr.'s birthday will frequently fall in the week following this Sunday, and so his ministry can be a contemporary example of what it means to follow Christ by being baptized with his baptism.

Preachers should note that for the next four Sundays the epistle and gospel lessons will be continuous readings from I Corinthians and Matthew and will not necessarily have any thematic connection. Beware of creative exegesis that proposes too much! If one is looking for connections, note that the Old Testament lessons are intended to be thematically connected to the gospel, and the psalm, as always, functions as a response to the Old Testament lesson.

Third Sunday After Epiphany

Old Testament Texts

Isaiah 9:1-4 has been chosen as the Old Testament lesson for this Sunday because it is quoted in Matthew 4:15-16. The larger text of Isaiah 9:2-7 was the Old Testament lesson for Christmas Day. Psalm 27:1, 4-9 is the first section of a psalm that presents the prayer of an innocent person who is being falsely accused and persecuted.

The Lesson: *Isaiah 9:1-4*

Salvation for Zebulun and Naphtali

Setting. The historical setting of Isaiah 9:1-4 is most probably in the latter third of the eighth century B.C.E. In 733-732 B.C.E., Tiglath-pileser conquered much of the northern territory of Israel and actually annexed the regions known as Zebulun and Naphtali to the Assyrian Empire (see II Kings 15:29). The prophet Isaiah's reference to the people of these regions as being in darkness most likely reflects the political realities of Assyrian occupation of the northern regions of Israel.

Structure. Isaiah 9:1-4 is not an independent unit of literature. The section should extend at least through the messianic proclamations in vv. 6-7 (see the comments for Year A, Christmas Eve/Day). The smaller unit of Isaiah 9:1-4 isolates the text from the messianic interpretation in vv. 6-7 and instead focuses on a reversal that will take place for dwellers in Galilee (the areas of Zubulun and Naphtali). This reversal is sharpened by the preceding unit of Isaiah 8:16-22, which sketches the darkness and gloom that accompanies the occupation of the Assyrian army. Notice how Isaiah 9:1 presupposes this unit when it begins, "But there will be no gloom for those who were in anguish." When the larger context is made clear, Isaiah 9:1-4 is probably best outlined in the following manner: v. 1 is a narrative introduction to a new salvation that God will bring to the northern regions of Israel; vv. 2-3 are an opening praise that fills out the radical character of God's new salvation through the contrasts of light and darkness; and v. 4 provides one reason for the reversal in fortunes of Zebulun and Naphtali by invoking the imagery of holy war.

Significance. As was already noted, when vv. 1-4 are detached from vv. 5-7 the point of focus must be on the people and the land, rather than on the messianic figure. The narrative introduction in v. 1 sets the tone for vv. 2-4. The former times can no longer determine the nature of reality for Naphtali and Zebulun, because God's actions toward them have changed. No longer will God treat them with contempt. Instead, in the new time, God will turn contempt into glory. Thus the new or latter time is characterized by celebration, because the overturning of political oppression is a sign of God's victory in holy war (for discussion of holy war in this text see Year A, Christmas Eve/Day). The preacher may wish to use this text in conjunction with the gospel lesson, where both the political and theological implications of God's salvation are taken up in the inauguration of Jesus' ministry.

The Response: *Psalm 27:1, 4-9*

"In This I Am Trusting."

Setting. The link between Psalm 27:1, 4-9 and Isaiah 9:1-4 is the motif of light that appears in each text as a metaphor of salvation. Psalm 27 divides into two parts. Verses 1-6 are a prayer of confidence by an individual, and vv. 7-14 are a lament. Scholars debate whether these sections of Psalm 27 constitute two independent psalms, or whether they are parts of a larger psalm. While the lectionary omits vv. 2-3, a look at the structure of the Psalm may provide a basis for their inclusion.

Structure. Psalm 27:1-9 can be structured in a number of different ways. The simple way is to divide the unit with vv. 1-3 functioning as an affirmation of the psalmist's faith in God, and vv. 4-9 as an expression of the psalmist's desire to live in communion with God. If we split the psalm in this way, then the final line in v. 3 stands out as providing transition. The line translates from the Hebrew quite literally as, "in this I am trusting."

Significance. The final line in v. 3 is translated in the NRSV, "yet I will be confident." This translation ties the line to the preceding one, which creates contrast in v. 3 between a military host encamping for the purpose of war and the psalmist's trust. But the verse raises the question of what exactly the psalmist is trusting in. If we read this final line of v. 3 in the larger context of vv. 1-3, then the answer must be found in v. 1—the psalmist believes that salvation rests in God and that this salvation is secure no matter how threatenting present experience may be.

The last line in v. 3 could also be read as a transition in the psalm. In this case the closing line, "in this I am trusting," (RSV) would be an introduction to what is following in vv. 4-9. When read in this way, the psalm provides much more information concerning the psalmist's trust. Verses 4-5 provide specific location for the psalmist's opening words of faith in v. 1. Not just any place can be equated with being the stronghold of God. Rather, God's sanctuary is the place of protection, for it is in the context of worship that the psalmist knows about God's salvation. This reality gives rise to the psalmist's one request in v. 4, which is never to be cut off from the presence of God in worship. All trials and threats in this life pale in the light of the goodness of God in the sanctuary. Consequently, to behold the beauty of God and to request divine direction in the Temple is the one thing that the psalmist cannot live without.

Psalm 27:4-9 concludes by shifting focus from general confessions about the security of God's salvation to the present time of the psalmist. Note how v. 6 begins, "Now my head is lifted up." The general statements of trust in God, even during threatening experience, give rise to worship in the present time. The message of the psalmist is clear. Abstract statements about trusting in God are made concrete in worshiping God within the sanctuary. God will no longer be hidden when the people shout forth with praise (v. 9). The same message is revealed in Psalm 22:3, where God inhabits or is enthroned on the praises of Israel.

New Testament Texts

Because these texts continue the sequential readings of ordinary time begun last week, any perceived thematic connections between the passages is more likely the product of the interpreter's imagination and speculation than the intention of the lectionary. Both texts do, however, record appeals: Paul calls for peace among the Corinthians and Jesus calls Simon Peter, Andrew, James, and John to be disciples.

The Epistle: *I Corinthians 1:10-18*

The Problem of Cliques in the Church

Setting. Having greeted the Corinthians (1:1-3) and having offered a thanksgiving prayer (vv. 4-9), Paul begins the "body" of his letter in vv. 10-17. The greeting reminded the Corinthians that they were part of the Church universal ("saints together with all those who in every place call on the name of our Lord Jesus Christ, both their Lord and ours"); and the thanksgiving prayer praised them (perhaps with tongue in cheek) for their spirituality and reminded them that it was the Lord Jesus Christ who was sustaining them in their lives as Christians. Having set these thoughts in the minds of the Corinthians, Paul appeals to members of factions in the congregation to be at peace with one another.

Structure. Paul's logic is both direct and sophisticated. He begins positively with an earnest appeal for congregational harmony (v. 10). Then, he brings up the problem of factions (vv. 11-12). This is excellent rhetorical strategy: calling first for the good motivates the needed changes that will dismantle the bad. Paul continues by asking a series of progressively more absurd rhetorical questions (1:13) and by making a set of seemingly shockingly cavalier remarks about baptism (vv. 14-16). Finally, the apostle declares his commission to preach and the purpose of his style of proclamation (v. 17). A sermon that adopted this movement could be very powerful: Call for the good. Criticize the bad. Expose the fallacy of the problem. State the proper position. And offer the theological validation for the point that you are advocating.

Significance. Paul addresses the problem of factions in the Corinthian church with their dissensions and quarreling. He expresses his astonishment and implies his disapproval. Although he states no resolution here, the implications of his full argument in the rest of the letter are present in these verses. In a nutshell, the Corinthians have formed groups and are trying to establish their spiritual superiority over one another by appealing to their relationship to various early Christian leaders. Paul's point is that such comparisons are wrong-spirited and wrong-headed, for it is God's work in the cross of Christ, not a minister's comeliness, that has the power to save.

Several items in the passage are striking: First, Paul's appeal is made "by (literally 'through' in Greek) the name of [the] Lord Jesus Christ.'' In this manner Paul locates the authority for his message in one other and greater than himself. Second, the call for the Corinthians to be united in mind and judgment is similar to the passage in Philippians 2 where the apostle calls for that congregation to have the very mind of Christ—meaning, harmony is achieved when humans move the focus off themselves and invest their lives in their Lord. Third, the presence of cliques that identify with this-or-that leader shows that even the earliest believers had differences, and the quarreling among the groups demonstrates the danger of Christians taking positions rather than living and moving under the direction of the risen Christ. Fourth, Paul's remarks about baptism show that when a practice becomes a problem, it may be a wineskin past its time. Fifth, Paul's last line in this passage is subtle and profound. The apostle offers a critique of preaching that has form but no fiber, style but no substance. He recognizes that sheer manipulative eloquence—which may produce striking results—is a medium that cannot bear the weight of the cross. Slick speech may slide away from the rough message of the cross.

The Gospel: *Matthew 4:12-23*

The Nature of Jesus' Ministry

Setting. Having recounted stories about Jesus' birth and his baptism by John, Matthew advances his story by telling of the beginning of Jesus' mission. Unfortunately the lectionary selections skip the account of Jesus' temptation described in Matthew 4:1-11, a passage that shows Jesus' profound struggle to determine how he will go about his ministry in pure service to God. This week's gospel reading has continuity with the previous week's lessons because of the mention of the arrest of John in 4:12. The passage tells briefly of Jesus' early work in order to set up the Sermon on the Mount in Matthew 5–7.

Structure. The text comprises three distinguishable units. Verses 12-17 indicate the motivation, the meaning, and the message of Jesus' ministry. Verses 18-22 tell of the call of the first disciples. And, v. 23 is disconnected from its true complement, 5:24-25. One may omit this verse without loss, but it may serve to fill out the picture of Jesus' ministry and the work to which he called the disciples. A sermon could easily focus on 4:12-17 (23?) or 4:18-22 (23?); in fact, such reduction of focus may enhance the coherence of the preaching, which otherwise would have to sweep across a broad field. Depending on the situation, one may choose to go deep or wide.

Significance. Matthew tells of the beginnings of Jesus' ministry in such a way that any possible perception of friction or competition between Jesus or John is reduced. Only after John's arrest does Jesus begin his work. Commentators often suggest that the geographical note concerning Jesus' withdrawing to Galilee indicates his desire to avoid political controversy at the outset of his ministry, but in fact, Galilee was under the governance of the same Herod Antipas who had arrested John. By moving to Galilee, Jesus actually steps into the void created by John's imprisonment. Thus he acts on the courage of the convictions demonstrated in the story of Jesus' temptations. Matthew's tracing of Jesus' travels is not a mere travelogue; indeed he tracks Jesus in order to make an important theological statement: as Jesus begins his ministry, he acts in such a manner that prophecy is fulfilled. This is clear from the reference to and quotation of Isaiah 8:23–9:1. Moreover, with the geographical notes and the quotation of Scripture, Matthew makes plain that the first movement of Jesus in ministry was related to the Gentiles, so that the universal scope of the gospel is explicit, not merely implicit, from the outset of Jesus' work. Remarkably, Luke's telling of the first full story of the beginning of Jesus' ministry, the account of Jesus' synagogue sermon and rejection at Nazareth, scores the same point in a very different way.

Verse 17 summarizes the content of the message of Jesus. He issues a call to repentance and identifies the imminence of the Kingdom of God and the motivation for such penitence. As is well known, repentance is more than remorse or guilt. Repentance is a change of heart, mind, and life's direction; it is a revamping of priorities and a reorientation of commitments. What makes such change possible? The presence and the power of God, specifically as God is at work in the world in Jesus Christ—the historical person and the risen, living Lord—in the advent of the Kingdom.

The phrase *the Kingdom of God* has been much studied and discussed. Often commentators and translators argue for the more dynamic phrase *the Reign of God*. Their point is that the phrase *the Kingdom of God* indicates the active Lordship of God as much as the place where God is Lord. Finding the right translation for both the dynamic and the localizing connotations of this phrase is not easy, and so in proclamation it is crucial to highlight both dimensions of the expression no matter which translation is selected. And, it is especially important to show the crucial relationship between the call to repentance and the initiative of God in the inbreaking of the Kingdom. (Some feminist readers also assert that the translation, *Kingdom,* is so patriarchal that it makes it very difficult for women to identify with the male kings and lords who rule the spaces.) Repentance follows, complies with, or results from the work of God. The Kingdom does not come as we repent; rather, as the Kingdom comes we repent.

The account of the call of four disciples in vv. 18-22 is a lesson about the Lordship of Jesus and the absolute demands of discipleship. It is impossible, even dangerous, to attempt historical and psychological explanations of this passage: for example, Jesus had met these men earlier and had made a deep impression on them. Such rationalizations explain the gospel right out of the text, and they are nothing more than speculations aimed at explaining the human, not the theological, dimensions of the story. From Matthew's telling of this story, Jesus calls disciples to set them about the same work to which he was himself devoted. Verse 23 tells what Jesus did in ministry. This story tells how and why Jesus called followers.

In their response, Peter, Andrew, James, and John are models of what it means to answer Jesus' call. Matthew tells us that both sets of brothers responded "immediately." Their reaction was sudden, and it was selfless. They left family and possessions to follow. We are not told that the disciples repented, but that they certainly experienced a profound change in their lives. Their activity was an abandonment of the normal forms of human security, in recognition of the authority of Jesus.

Epiphany 3: The Celebration

This Sunday will generally fall during the Week of Prayer for Christian Unity (January 18-25), and so the epistle, because it addresses the problem of division among the Corinthian Christians, is particularly fitting for this day. In our day we can relate to the circumstances where the followers of outstanding leaders like Peter and Paul are listed among those who have become part of the problem in Corinth, because party lines appear to have been drawn around them (and others).

The dates for the observance of the Unity Octave (eight days, actually, rather than a week) were not chosen arbitrarily, but because they began and ended with feast days in honor of Peter and Paul respectively. Prior to the reforms of Vatican II, January 18 was the feast of St. Peter's Chair at Rome. The intent of the celebration was questionable as an ecumenical event, however, from the Protestant point of view, because, as one missal commentary put it, "this feast can be considered a liturgical evidence of the primacy of honor and jurisdiction attached to the chair of Rome." (*St. Andrew Daily Missal,* Dom Gaspar Lefebvre, ed. [St. Paul: E. M. Lohmann Co., 1953], p. 612) The feast was dropped in the missal of Paul VI, but nothing was put in its place, so for Roman Catholics, the Unity Octave lost the symbolism of the balance between Peter and Paul. Lutherans and Episcopalians have attempted to restore the balance by instituting a new feast on that day in honor of the Confession of Peter with the gospel lesson being Matt. 16:13-19. January 25, a much older festival in honor of the Conversion of St. Paul, is still widely observed across denominational lines. The observance of these days marking the Unity Octave implies that the unity of the Church is dependent upon an ongoing conversation between Peter and Paul and their contemporary disciples.

For more than a decade, ecumenism has fared worse than the weather, since it is difficult even to find anyone talking about it, let alone doing anything about it! Today is a chance to talk about it, to draw new images of a united Christian witness, to dare to ask if Jesus' teaching about needing to lose our lives in order to save them applies to our denominational identities as well. The theme of unity also proceeds naturally from a discussion of baptism if the sermons of the two previous Sundays have dealt with that topic.

Planners of worship will benefit from two books compiled by John Carden for the World Council of Churches: *With All God's People: The New Ecumenical Prayer Cycle* and *With All God's People: Orders of Service*. Both are available from the World Council of Churches, 475 Riverside Drive, Room 915, New York, NY 10115-0050.

Fourth Sunday After Epiphany

Old Testament Texts

The Old Testament texts are a call for us to act in accordance with the reality that we know is true. Micah 6:1-8 makes this point through a legal confrontation between God and Israel, while Psalm 37:1-11 presents a series of wisdom sayings that are meant to bring the reality of God more clearly into focus by encouraging us to adopt the moral way of life.

The Lesson: *Micah 6:1-8*

Controversy in the Congregation

Setting. Micah 6:1-8 uses the imagery of dispute as the setting for the prophetic oracle. The setting of the disputation or controversy is common in prophetic speech (see for example, Isaiah 1:2, Hosea 4:1-3, Jeremiah 2:4-12) and has been researched extensively by biblical scholars. Some scholars emphasize the setting of the courtroom to interpret these texts. In this analogy, the mountains are called into the courtroom as witnesses to hear the case (v. 1), the defendants are summoned to arise and plead their case (v. 1), the Lord is either the judge or prosecutor who states the case to the witnesses (that is, presents a "controversy," v. 2), which is then followed by the questions and answers of prosecutor and defendant (vv. 3-8).

Other scholars assert that this form of controversy has roots in the larger world of ancient Near Eastern international law, where legal treaties were used to spell out the relationships between powerful monarchs and lesser states. This larger background of international law, which makes for fascinating study in its own right, has then been laid over the courtroom scene in Micah 6:1-8, so that the text is interpreted as a dispute over a broken treaty.

A third approach, which will be the point of departure for the present interpretation is that the disputation or controversy is located in the worshiping community (rather than the secular courtroom). Note how the setting in the worshiping community is emphasized in vv. 6-7 when the defendant responds. These verses use the formulaic language of a cultic entrance liturgy in which the worshiper inquires how to approach God in the sanctuary. When Micah 6:1-8 is read within the setting of worship, the imagery is not of a judge, but of a priest who rises up to denounce apostasy (a religious form of injustice) and, in the process, picks a fight with the other leaders—in the name of God, of course! In such controversies the priest crosses over the imaginary line to become a prophet.

Structure. As noted, the setting of the secular courtroom in Micah 6:1-8 is problematic in several ways. The apparent transition from courtroom language to cultic language is accompanied by a change in speaker: from God or prosecutor to Israel or defendant. When we add that v. 8 introduces yet another speaker (perhaps the prophet functioning in a priestly role), then it is more accurate to think of the worshiping community that is assembled and enmeshed in controversy over who is allowed to approach the Lord if apostasy and wickedness are rampant in cult and commerce. The controversy separates into four parts.

1. Announcement of guilt (vv. 1-2)
2. Lamentation (vv. 3-5)
3. Confession by the Accused (vv. 6-7)
4. Absolution via the prophet (v. 8)

Significance. Verses 1-5: The announcement of guilt in vv. 1-2 underscores the culpability of Israel in not living up to the obligations of the covenant that was established between God and the people. The lamentations in v. 3 imply a breakdown of the relationship of God and Israel, while the recitation of salvation history in vv. 4-5 make it clear that God has been faithful and that the problem of apostasy lies elsewhere.

Verses 6-7: The language of lamentation and grief gives way to cultic language of sacrifice in Israel's response in vv. 6-7. Guilt is acknowledged, and the acknowledgment is followed by a series of cultic questions about purgation that have an almost frantic aura about them. Piety is not a problem in this text. The three questions of the accused ascend in intensity, probing how a right relationship with God can be reestablished. What can I do? Should I offer a burnt offering of a one-year-old calf? How about one thousand rams with ten thousand rivers of oil? What if I sacrifice my own flesh and blood? As the questions indicate, the religious piety quickly ascends to the level of absurdity. Who has a thousand rams? What would ten thousand rivers of oil actually be? What parents are going to sacrifice their child? The shift in language from guilt and lamentation in vv. 3-5 to mere cultic activity in vv. 6-7 points to the problem that underlies the controversy raging in the worshiping community. The congregation thinks that some kind of action can rectify the situation, when in fact no good deed (no matter how pious or culticly based) can bring about the transformation central to God's salvation. To know God's salvation means that one already knows this to be the truth. Thus the response of the accused—although frantic in its piety—simply underscores the problem that the prophet Micah wishes to address—that Israel has lost sight of God's salvation.

Verse 8: Thus the prophet returns in v. 8 and virtually ignores the response of the accused. Rather than keeping the discussion at the objective level of cultic activity, namely, ''With what shall I come before the LORD . . . ?'' the prophet focuses on the person in the light of the past reality of God's salvation. Verse 5 concluded the anguished review of salvation history by underscoring how these events were meant for Israel to ''know the saving acts of the LORD.'' Verse 8 begins at this point, when the prophet answers the frantic cultic questions by stating that Israel already knows what is required. Salvation is not doing more things, it is being the transformed people that God has brought into existence. Thus the prophet's call for Israel to do justice and to love steadfast kindness is not first and foremost a call for human actions that might atone us before God in a court. Rather, they are qualities that we acquire from God through salvation (and thus already know), and in living them out we walk with God.

135

The setting in the cult should prevent any interpreter from asserting that Micah, as an eighth century "ethical" prophet, is against the covenantal demands or obligations of the cult. If anything, the text is just the reverse, for it is only in worship that we "know the saving acts of the LORD." The prophet's point is that there is no salvation outside the worshiping community. Through this community at worship, we learn about and participate in actions and rituals that must reach beyond these boundaries and influence all aspects of our lives. We must act in accordance with the salvation that we know to be true.

When preaching on this lesson, the pastor might seize the opportunity to address the controversies that churn within congregations and denominations, to address the question: who is allowed to approach the Lord? What does the Lord require? Another risky way into the same sermon is to ask, What is apostasy, and who is guilty of it?

The Response: *Psalm 15*

Encouragement for Living the Moral Life

Setting. Psalm 15 is best characterized as an entrance liturgy (see Psalm 24 for an additional example of this genre). The description "entrance liturgy" is meant quite literally. The psalm most likely functioned as a litany to inform worshipers of what was required of them to enter the Jerusalem Temple.

Structure. The question and answer format of Psalm 15 provides the central clue to its structure. Verse 1 poses the question to God concerning who may enter. This question is probably communal in nature and not being placed by an individual. Verses 2-5a provide the divine answer by listing a series of characteristics that create a profile of the person of God. Verse 5b concludes the psalm with a promise that those who fulfill the moral requirements of God will experience the richness of life.

Significance. Psalm 15 provides an important counterpoint of Micah 6:1-8. Micah underscores how salvation is not first and foremost about ethics. Rather, it is rooted in God's transformation. Once this central reality is established, the entrance liturgy in Psalm

15 provides the other side of the issue—namely, that the transformed life of the people of God will inevitably result in moral conduct that is in harmony with God's character.

New Testament Texts

These texts complement each other. Paul writes of the distinctive manner in which God works for salvation, and Matthew presents Jesus' teachings about the characteristics of his disciples. Both passages are extraordinarily rich in exploring the depths of Christian life.

The Epistle: *1 Corinthians 1:18-31*

God's Peculiar Ways

Setting. Having declared in the opening of the body of the letter that elegant proclamation may indeed empty the cross of Christ of its true power (1:17), Paul moves in this passage to meditate on the striking, even peculiar (from a human point of view), way that God wrought salvation for humankind.

Structure. In v. 18 Paul articulates his thesis, which he justifies through the quotation of scripture (1:19). Then, in vv. 20-25 Paul employs various rhetorical strategies—questions, declarations, juxtapositions—to emphasize that God's ways, though unexpected, are superior. Then, in vv. 26-31 Paul turns specifically to the Corinthians. He uses their own backgrounds as evidence of the veracity of his claims, ultimately to turn their attention away from themselves (the cause of controversy) and toward God (the source of salvation).

Significance. Paul teaches that God works in direct defiance of human standards. Moreover, God's work is powerful, so it incapacitates and reverses the established values of this world. Paul declares this as fact and argues to establish his case.

Verse 18 is an arresting statement, articulating one of Paul's central theological convictions. Paul says (I have translated and schematized the statement):

> "For the word of the cross
>   a. to the ones who are perishing
>   b. is folly;
> but
>   a. to us who are being saved
>   b. it is the power of God."

He contrasts two groups: (1) those who are perishing and (2) those who are being saved, and he numbers himself and the Corinthians in the latter group. The criterion for the separation of these groups is the cross—specifically the word (meaning, the preaching) of the cross. The cross has different meanings for the groups. To those who are perishing it is folly, but to those being saved it is (one would expect in the structural juxtapositions of Paul's remark to read "the wisdom of God," but instead one finds) the power of God. This is the apostle's "theology of the cross." Paul deliberately shapes a remark to drive home the point that the cross is the power of God that saves a group of humans. In other words, Paul argues that it is not human activity—even as a comprehension of God's ways—but divine action that saves humanity.

Paul backs up his point with a quotation of Isaiah 29:14, which uses the verb *thwart* rather than the verb *conceal,* which actually occurs in the Septuagint. In short, Paul modifies the text to make it more applicable to his argument. He gives scriptural precedent for God's work in the cross of Christ and does not merely provide a prooftext. Paul's use of the Bible shows that scripture is authoritative, essential, and of penultimate significance. The text serves "the word of the cross," and the preacher's ultimate concern is with the gospel, not the text.

In the following verses, Paul jabs at those who may differ with his teaching. He asks after the wise, the scribe, and the debater "of this age." His phrase, "of this age," locates where human wisdom originates. Then, Paul talks about what God has done in and through the crucified Christ. Paul's argument contends that humans do not reason their way to God, because God saves by the (word of) the cross of Christ, which by this world's standards is "folly." The point:

Salvation is God's activity. Preaching Christ as crucified brings a crisis of separation. To deny God's saving work shows bondage to "this world"; whereas, those who believe the gospel are called, which shows they are grasped by the power of God. Believers know the crucified Christ as God's wisdom.

Verse 25 ends this section with an epigrammatic truth, which Paul applies to the Corinthian situation in the following verses (26-31). Worldly wisdom judges the wisdom of God to be foolishness, but, in fact, the supposed foolishness of God renders worldly wisdom into true foolishness. Thus one sees the power of the wisdom of God.

In vv. 26-31 Paul calls for the Corinthians to consider themselves—both before their being called and after their calling. Bluntly stated, before their call the Corinthians were nobodies, but after God called them they became instruments of God's power with Christ Jesus as the source of their lives. Paul summarizes his argument with another quotation of scripture to tell the Corinthians if they boast, they should boast of (literally "by" or "in") the Lord.

The Gospel: *Matthew 5:1-12*

The Blessings of Discipleship

Setting. In Matthew 4:24-25 one learns that Jesus attracted a large following as he went about his ministry. This week's text opens with Jesus looking upon that following and, in turn, teaching them about the characteristics of his disciples. Verses 1-12 are formally the beginning of the famous section of Matthew's Gospel called "The Sermon on the Mount" (Matthew 5:1–7:28). The lectionary reading is located appropriately in ordinary time, for it is in the ordinary times of life that one needs direction for knowing what it means to be a follower of Jesus Christ. Here, like a Celtic priest, Christ blesses the hearers.

Structure. Verses 1-2 introduce the well-known Beatitudes in vv. 3-12. The material is quite deliberately structured, as can be seen from a careful comparison of this passage with the comparable text in Luke 6:20-23. There are four pronouncements common to the two Gospels, and Matthew's list contains five beatitudes without parallel in Luke. Luke's text seems more primitive than Matthew's balanced and elaborate passage. Matthew offers two sets of sayings structured in an A/B/A/B pattern that cohere by beginning and ending with the line "for theirs is the kingdom of heaven," and both end with a stated concern for "righteousness":

A poor in spirit, for theirs is the kingdom of heaven

B mourn

A meek

B hunger and thirst for righteousness

A merciful

B pure in heart

A peacemakers

B persecuted for righteousness . . . for theirs is the kingdom of heaven

The final beatitude, which is somewhat different in form and tone, epitomizes the beatitude for the persecuted.

Significance. Matthew tells the reader that Jesus "went up the mountain." He does not name the mountain, however, for it is of more symbolic than geographical importance. In the Old Testament, mountains are regularly the place where divine revelation occurs. One thinks immediately of Horeb, Sinai, and Zion. A precise identification is not necessary, but the Beatitudes begin the sermon in a manner similar to the way the Ten Commandments introduce the Law, so that the precursor of Matthew's mountain may well be Sinai. Nevertheless, on a place where one expects a divine communication, Jesus sits (the normal, authoritative teaching posture of his time) and then speaks.

Even the basic pertinent information for interpretation of the Beatitudes is voluminous, so the following remarks focus on matters to stimulate thoughts for preaching. First, throughout the Beatitudes, Jesus' address is to "you" in the plural Greek form. These relate to community life, not merely personal piety. Jesus' words describe the life that believers are to live in relation to one another and to the world.

Second, in v. 3, Matthew "spiritualized" the concept of the poor (as he does mourning, hunger, and thirst in the subsequent lines), moving beyond a literal sense. In Israel, a class of people, often genuinely impoverished, called themselves "the poor." The term designated a style of piety that allowed nothing other than God to be the basis of security. Being poor, having nothing, was celebrated as an opportunity for absolute, radical dependence upon God. Such piety was not passive, however; for faith was no placebo. Persons fully committed to God were extremely free. One thinks of John the Baptist and Jesus as examples of such piety. Third, from the statement in v. 4 itself, it is not immediately clear how Matthew interpreted mourning as a spiritual disposition. The parallel line in v. 6 mentions righteousness as the object of hunger and thirst, so that perhaps those mourning are grieved by their lack of righteousness. In any case, the promise to the mourners is striking: they shall be comforted. This line contains a common phenomenon in biblical literature, the "divine passive." The unnamed actor in such a text is God. The use of the passive came originally through the concern of pious Jews to avoid using God's name or even referring to God directly. Verse 6 is quite similar to this line, though its sense is more straightforward.

Fourth, the reference to the meek in v. 5 recalls Psalm 37:11. "Meekness" is akin to "poverty" in much of the Old Testament, and as such, it refers to the submission of human will to the divine. Fifth, v. 7 foreshadows the words of the Lord's Prayer, "Forgive us our debts, as we forgive our debtors." The translation, "for they shall obtain mercy," may be misleading. This does not mean that we gain mercy by being merciful; rather, grace begets grace. Those experiencing divine mercy live merciful lives that bespeak the mercy which they themselves receive. Sixth, the reference in v. 8 to "the pure in heart" indicates persons who are single-mindedly devoted to God. Thus the promise "they shall see God." Søren Kierkegaard wrote eloquently of this notion in *Purity of Heart*, as did Jonathan Edwards in *True Virtue*. This line is a positive critique of divided loyalties that compromise complete devotion to God. Seventh, in v. 9 "peacemakers" names persons actively engaged in the pursuit of peace. Clearly they are doing God's will, as though they were, and in fact are, God's own children. Eighth, v. 10 blesses those "persecuted

141

for righteousness' sake'' and promises them ''the kingdom of heaven.'' This statement is consistent with all that went before, but the pronouncement alters the tone of the passage, as it introduces the idea of experiencing persecution as a Christian. This frank recognition that true piety does not guarantee an increased popularity is a sobering reminder that Christian faith is not a rosy-glowing, saccharin-sweet piety. True faith, Jesus says, may be tough and costly. The more elaborate statement in vv. 11-12 develops this idea and forms a crucial parallel between suffering for righteousness' sake and suffering for Jesus' sake.

Epiphany 4: The Celebration

The preacher should take seriously the comment made earlier about the lesson from Micah: ''Salvation is not doing more things; it is being the transformed people that God has brought into existence.'' Resist, then, the temptation to use Micah and Matthew as occasions for exhortation to improvement in virtue, in humility and meekness, and emphasize instead the character that God gives to the baptized community, a character into which we grow through our active participation in the celebration of Word and Sacrament. P. T. Forsythe's advice to preachers over fifty years ago could not be more relevant today:

> Do not tell people how they ought to feel toward Christ. It is just what they cannot do. Preach a Christ that will make them feel as they ought. That is objective preaching. The tendency and fashion of the present moment is all in the direction of subjectivity. People welcome sermons of a more or less psychological kind, which go into the analysis of the soul or of society. They will listen gladly to sermons on character-building, for instance; and in the result they will get to think of nothing else but their own character. They will be the builders of their own character; which is a fatal thing. Learn to commit your soul and the building of it to One who can keep it and build it as you never can. [*The Work of Christ* (London: Independent Press, 1938), p. 4]

In keeping with the previous week's emphasis on Christian unity, liturgical planners may wish to follow a pattern of Orthodox worship and use the Beatitudes as part of the opening rite. The liturgist recites or sings each beatitude and the congregation responds to each with a formula such as, "Lord, have mercy upon us, and grant us this blessing." After v. 12, the Prayer of St. John Chrysostom (No. 412 in *The United Methodist Hymnal;* p. 102 in *The Book of Common Prayer*) might be used in unison, and the service would then proceed to an anthem or the reading of the first lesson.

Fifth Sunday After Epiphany

Old Testament Texts

Both Old Testament texts underscore the importance of integrating faith into all aspects of our lives. Isaiah 58:1-12 explores the inherent interrelationship between worship and ethics, while Psalm 112:1-9 (10) functions in praise of godliness.

The Lesson: *Isaiah 58:1-9a (9b-12)*

Worship and Ethics

Setting. Isaiah 58:1-12 is a critique of worship. The opening line is a question by the worshiper, asking why God is absent from worship or at the very least why God is not responding to acts of worship. After this question the passage shifts to an extended divine discourse in vv. 3-12 that is meant to answer the question. Much of the divine speech appears to be a rejection of Israel's worship and a call for righteous ethical action. Note, for example, the divine judgment on fasting in vv. 3b-5 and the call for ethical activity in vv. 6-7. Criticisms of worship, similar to Isaiah 58:1-12 have influenced our understanding of Old Testament prophets, and these ideas have shaped our views of worship. In particular, texts of this type have given rise to an idealization of prophets as individualistic outsiders who critically evaluate the status quo (those who make up the worshiping community) with a call for righteous ethical action. The result of this kind of idealization of prophets is that worship and ethical action are often pitted against each other, which gives rise to an interpretation of a text like Isaiah 58:1-12 as demeaning worship in favor of good sound ethical application. This line of interpretation (prophetic ethics against the worshiping community) is unfortunate, for nothing could be further from the interaction of prophet and community in Israel. Prophets frequently criticize the worshiping community because of their belief that sound ethical action requires revelation, which is only possible in the context of worship. Thus prophets are not rejecting worship in favor of proper ethical activity. Instead, a text like Isaiah 58:1-12 must be interpreted as a prophetic call for authentic worship so that the community is able to be ethical and obedient to the covenantal law.

Structure. Isaiah 58:1-2 presents an opening divine judgment of worship in which transgression is declared (v. 1) and worship without acts of righteousness is condemned (v. 2). This judgment provides background for vv. 3-12, which divide into vv. 3-4, vv. 5-9a, vv. 9b-12. Each of these sections is internally structured around questions or conditions, and answers. The first section begins with a question by the worshiper concerning divine absence in worship (v. 3a) and an initial response by God (v. 4). The second section is made up entirely of divine speech in which God both asks the questions (vv. 5-7) and provides the answers (vv. 8-9a). The third section establishes conditions that God has offered the community, with consequences resulting. A closer look at this structure will bring to light the inherent link between worship and ethical action that is at the center of Isaiah 58:3-12.

Significance. The opening question by the worshiper in v. 3a gives rise to the remainder of the text. The worshiper notes how the community has gone through the proper acts of worship (fasting) with appropriate piety (''humble ourselves''), and yet God appears to be indifferent. Thus the question in v. 3a is really a lament being made in the context of worship. The initial divine answer in vv. 3b-4 could not be more direct. Fasting or worship is functioning to fulfill the needs or pleasure of the worshiper (v. 3b) and thus it is not being integrated into any activity outside of the setting of the Temple (v. 3b-4a). The divine assessment of this situation is that such activity isn't worship at all. Consequently the voice of the community could not possibly be heard on high (v. 4b).

The setting of the Temple continues in vv. 5-9a, but a very different dynamic begins to develop beyond the lament of v. 3a because God rather than the worshiper, asks the questions. The divine questions transform the setting into genuine worship, because the questions actually function as revelation for the worshiper, which makes ethical activity possible. The divine questions are of two kinds. The first three questions in v. 5 imply a negative answer in describing the worship activity of the people. These questions underscore how worship is not meant to fulfill the needs of the worshiper. The two questions in vv. 6-7 imply a positive answer, and as such they are revelation that provides the content for worship. The first question in v. 6 underscores how the salvation of God is a reversal of the power structures of this world—those in slavery are freed, yokes are broken. The second question in v. 7 outlines the new relationships that emerge with God's salvation—food is shared, homeless are housed, and in general we do not hide ourselves from other humans in need.

Verses 8-9a provide consequences that will result from ethical behavior in the worshiping community, and as such they provide an answer to the preceding questions of God. If the worshipers see the revelation in the questions that God has just asked, then two things will happen. First, the worshiping community will live the upright ethical life outside of the sanctuary (v. 8). And second, God will continue to be present in their worship (v. 9).

Further consequences to right living (vv. 9b-10a), which is defined as feeding the hungry and comforting the sick, will result in a metaphorical vision of a restored social order that will last for many generations of safe cities and clean streets.

The message in Isaiah 58:1-12 is not a choice between sound ethics or worship. Rather, it is call for authentic worship, where the revelation of God (in this case a series of divine questions and conditions) determines the content of reality and the character of the community. When this happens it cannot help flowing outside of the sanctuary and being translated into ethical action.

The Response: *Psalm 112:1-9 (10)*

In Praise of Godliness

Setting. Psalm 112:1-9 could be read as an extension of Isaiah 58:1-12, because it shifts from the setting of the sanctuary to praise ethical action that flows from worship. Psalm 112 is an acrostic wisdom psalm that is a counterpart to Psalm 111. Both psalms follow the alphabet in structuring their poetic lines, and they share some of the same motifs. For example, the phrase "his righteousness endures for ever" occurs in Psalm 111:1 and 112:3, and the motif of being established or steady is employed in Psalm 111:8 and Psalm 112:8. The difference between the two psalms is that the attributes used to describe God in Psalm 111 are applied to the godly person in Psalm 112. This larger interrelationship between Psalms 111–112 should be kept in mind when interpreting the praise of godliness in Psalm 112.

Structure. The acrostic structure determines much of the internal arrangement of Psalm 112. The lectionary text includes neither the opening praise of God and the blessing of the godly person (vv. 1-3) nor the concluding contrast to the wicked person (v. 10).

Significance. Psalm 112:4-9 can be read in two different ways. The ambiguity arises from the Hebrew in v. 4. The "light" that "rises in the darkness" could be a reference to God as light, as he is referred to frequently in the Old Testament, or it could be a reference to the godly person. This ambiguity is carried through into the second line of v. 4. If the light is a description of God, then the qualities of "graciousness, mercy, and righteousness" also refer to God. The RSV has interpreted the verse this way and thus added the words, "the LORD" to v. 4b. You should note that these words do not occur in the Hebrew text, and are eliminated in the NRSV. *Light* could just as well be a reference to the godly person who is then being described as "gracious, merciful, and righteous" in v. 4b. If v. 4 is a description of God, then Psalm 112:1-9 separates between v. 4 (God) and vv. 5-9 (godly person). If v. 4 is a description of the godly person then there is no separation within the unit. The use of *light* to describe the ethical activity of the godly person in Isaiah 58:8 may prompt you to favor the latter reading for this week. But to push the distinction between the two interpretations of the verse may actually cause us to miss the point of the psalm. The very ambiguity of God as light and our ethical action as light is probably what the psalm is about. If we receive the blessing of God in worship and absorb God's light, then we cannot help reflecting that light in all of our activity. In other words, the one blessed becomes a blessing to others. Read in this way, the psalm is advocating the same point as found in Isaiah 58:1-12.

New Testament Texts

The texts have one thing in common this week: Each has two distinct parts that are related to each other but that, in fact, form distinguishable thought units.

The Epistle: *I Corinthians 2:1-12 (13-16)*

The Mystery of God and How It's Known

Setting. Paul continues to argue against the spiritual boasting of the Corinthians by illustrating the continuity between his apostolic message ("the cross") and style of ministry ("weakness" and "fear and trembling"). The reflection in the previous section of the letter declared the saving work of God and, then, focused on the Corinthians to illustrate the veracity of the statements about God. Paul continues his argument in 2:1-16, but he moves through personal illustration to consider Christian epistemology—namely, how believers know what they know about God.

Structure. Paul illustrates the claim that God's standards are neither those "of humans" nor "of this age" by writing of his own ministry (vv. 1-5). In turn, Paul comments on his work and the failure of "the rulers of this age" to comprehend God's ways (vv. 6-9); and then he meditates on God's self-revelation through the Spirit (vv. 9-11). The remainder of I Corinthians 2 applies Paul's teaching to the Christian community (vv. 12-13), and then, Paul becomes more universal in this orientation when reflecting on "the unspiritual one" versus "the spiritual one" (vv. 14-16).

Significance. Paul's exposition of his apostolic message and ministry begins in vv. 1-2 with personal remarks, which illustrate his argument by referring to the continuity between the form or style of his ministry and the content or substance of the gospel (vv. 1-2). For information, the RSV translation "the testimony of God" is altered to "the mystery of God" in the NRSV in accordance with the best textual evidence, so Paul is concerned directly with the unfathomable nature of God's salvific work rather than with commentary on that activity. He comes directly to this issue in vv. 10-11. Verse 2 declares that Paul's approach was deliberate. He is not saying, "I preached the cross only—instead of the cross + something else"; rather, he avers that he laid aside all devices for persuasion and proclaimed the cross without human frills. This idea generates the remarks that come in vv. 6-16.

In vv. 3-5 Paul remarks on the continuity of his message and his demeanor. In his self-portrait, Paul uses common Old Testament language to create the image of "fear and trembling" in awareness of the presence of God. This is not mere terror but genuine reverence. Similarly, *weakness* means "without human power." In contrast, Paul says his message was "in demonstration of the Spirit and of power." What does this mean? The Greek is ambiguous. Paul could mean either that his speech demonstrated the Spirit and power or that his speech allowed the Spirit and power to show themselves in working through his message. Verse 5 makes the latter meaning preferable when Paul clarifies his point, saying that he worked as he did—(literally) "in order that your faith may not be in human wisdom but in God's power" (which, recall, is "foolishness" in this world's eyes).

In turn, Paul comments on the wisdom of God and the spiritual discernment of Christians—or, on the operation of revelation. Because of the opening phrase of v. 6 ("Yet among the mature we do speak wisdom,") commentators ask whether Paul contradicts his earlier remarks. Does he have a two-leveled message? The problem takes us back to theidea of "the word of the cross" in 1:18. Is this a message about the cross, or a message the cross implies, or both? Clearly, Paul unpacks "the cross" throughout his letters, applying its meaning to the lives of his readers. The cross is not only something that happened to Jesus, it is that which affects—or effects!—the lives of Christians. It is unlikely that Paul had special teaching for some. He could, however, explicate more to some than to others. Verse 7 summarizes what the depths of Paul's message were, and v. 8 comments upon its availability, or nonavailability. But, v. 8 raises a question, "How can this be?" How could "the leaders of this age" miss God's work? Verse 9 answers with a scriptural precedent (although the reference cannot be identified with precision). Verse 10 clarifies this cryptic quotation, saying that the deeper communication of God's truth is possible and takes place "through the Spirit." Having made this statement, Paul forms a further argument on the principle "like by like." A person is the only one who knows the inner secrets of herself or himself. It is likewise with God. Here Paul speaks of this inner or thorough knowledge in terms of "spirit"—first, "of humanity"; then, "of God." God is known by humans as God's Spirit makes God known. Worldly social, political, or religious status is not a guarantee of true perception of God. Indeed, God's strange ways are almost deliberately oblivious to such standing. "The rulers of this age" did not recognize Christ because God's Spirit did not reveal God's ways to them.

The Gospel: *Matthew 5:13-20*

Christians as Salt and Light

Setting. In the wake of the Beatitudes, Matthew offers a collection of the sayings of Jesus to explicate the meaning of discipleship. Mark contains similar statements (salt [9:49-50] and light [4:21]) in widely separated contexts, but the sayings are made as riddle-parables, not pronouncements, to guide the disciples in understanding their call. As in Mark, Luke separates the words on salt (14:34-35) and light (8:16), but Luke agrees with Matthew against Mark in having Jesus utter these sayings publicly to the multitude rather than only to the inner circle of disciples. This agreement suggests that Matthew is responsible for bringing these teachings together and for setting them in the Sermon on the Mount, so that in Matthew these statements function as general teaching on the nature of Christian discipleship.

Structure. Matthew's material focuses on salt and light, followed by an exhortation to zealously keep the law and live out the justice that is evident in the prophets. There are five separate pronouncements concerning salt and light. (1) Verse 13 deals with salt in three moves: positive observation, potential problem, and warning. (2) Verse 14*a* makes a pronouncement on light. (3) Verse 14*b* is a metaphor about a city set on a hill. (4) Verse 15 is another metaphor—about light. And

(5) verse 16 is an admonition to faithful living using the metaphorical language of light. A similar admonition concerning righteous living is found in verse 20, which is the result of behavior modified by every stroke of the law. Believers are to respect the Law, teach its way, and embody its true intention. In that way believers are followers of Jesus.

Significance. Commentators often study these verses by trying to recover the original setting of the teaching in the ministry of Jesus. The range of suggestions about original settings shows the precarious nature of this endeavor. Moreover, analysis of Jesus' *Sitz-im-Leben* can obscure the meaning of the text in its canonical form. One should not disparage research in the history of traditions, but one should not substitute such investigation for an encounter with the content of the text.

Jesus' remark is emphatic: "You are the salt of the world." The second person plural pronoun is unnecessary in Greek since the verb carries the person and number of the subject in its ending. The sense of the statement is "You yourselves are the salt of the earth!" Jesus' teaching is as much a commission as an observation; thus the warning about salt that becomes insipid. The words of caution may be problematic even for a fledgling chemist, since NaCl (sodium chloride = salt) is a compound incapable of passive degeneration. But salt in ancient Palestine was harvested in an adulterated form that contained other natural substances that could and did "go bad," so that the salt became useless. Worthless salt, Jesus says, is thrown out—his point: Faith gone to pot is worse than useless, it is deplorable.

Disciples also are charged to be "the light of the world." The words are suggestive, for Israel commonly referred to itself as "the light of the world," and the Gospel according to John calls Jesus "the light of the world." The phrase designates the agents of God at work for the salvation of the world. Christians are to be God's light—showing forth God's ways, bringing illumination, and exposing wrong.

The next saying about the city on the hill tells us that some things are obvious simply by virtue of their existence and position. In terms of discipleship, the saying declares that followers of Jesus are conspicuous because they "stand out." Jesus is neither granting us privilege nor admonishing us to eccentricity. He says to be what we are—disciples, whose ways are being taught in the entirety of the Sermon—and we will be recognizable.

The subsequent saying makes a similar point about the inevitable explicitness of discipleship. Lest one translate faith into purely private piety, Jesus states that a purely personal faith defies the purposes of the gracious gift of discipleship with which God has blessed us. Discipleship without visible consequences is ridiculous, like a lit lamp under a basket.

The final saying takes its point of departure from the previous word about light. This teaching is a forceful admonition to "let your light shine. . . . " Clearly the purpose of discipleship is the glorification of God. Christians live "Christian lives," not for self-aggrandizement, but for the sake of God. Such is true piety.

Jesus speaks about "the Law and the prophets." Ancient Jews would have understood that he was speaking about the so-called books of Moses and the collection of the writings of the prophets of Israel. These two bodies of literature were thought of in relation to each other in Judaism as text and interpretation. Thus in v. 19 Jesus can say only "Law," but he is still concerned with the same items named in v. 18. The teaching of Jesus concerning the Law steers a middle course between the extremes of legalism and libertinism. He does not speak as an iconoclast, advocating that we dispense with the Law as we freely live a life of faith, and he does not insist that we slavishly follow the Law as if it were a rule book for faithful living. Jesus says instead that he came to "fulfill" the Law. In brief, he means that his life and ministry embody the heart, the essence, or the intention of the larger body of writings. As Jesus lived and taught, on the one hand, he personified God's standards; and, on the other, as he spoke and acted he brought to fulfillment the words of the prophets of old. These verses simply state what Matthew is concerned to communicate throughout his Gospel—namely, that in Jesus Christ all of God's purposes and all of Israel's expectations find their realization.

Remarkable consistency is evident between the person and work of Jesus Christ and the ways and purposes of God, which had been made known to Israel throughout the nation's history. Thus in v. 19 we are warned against having a lax attitude toward "the commandments." Indeed, Jesus declares that our standing in "the kingdom of heaven" is directly related to how faithfully we live and teach God's ways. Having advocated faithfulness to God's purposes, Jesus continues in v. 20 with a negative comparison designed to advocate genuine devotion to God, not merely following the rules. Scholars debate the background of this verse. Some suggest that the line reflects the context of the historical debate between Jesus and the Pharisees over the interpretation of the Hebrew Law, but others associate the degree of repudiation of the Pharisees with the later life of the Church in Matthew's time, when Christians were in conflict and competition with Pharisees. A final decision on this matter may be impossible, so one is better advised to direct whatever remarks are to be made in proclamation to Christians, as admonition, rather than against non-Christians as condemnation.

These sayings call us to a life of discipleship that will have visible consequences in the world, and we are told that the true goal of our activity is the glory of God. We do not work for approval—a kind of Protestant work-ethic righteousness, and we do not rest assured of our salvation in a passive, ineffective life of piety. We live boldly for God and to God's glory.

Epiphany 5: The Celebration

In the light of the commentary on the psalm for today, it is preferable to use the entire psalm rather than the selected verses. If the NRSV is used, v. 4 begins with "they," which can only be understood from the first three verses.

The conjunction of the Old Testament lesson and the gospel can give rise to an examination of worship as a process of Christian formation. The assertion in the exegesis that "worship is not meant merely to fulfill the needs of the worshiper" will not find a welcome hearing among those who evaluate Sunday morning only in terms of education ("I learned something new today"), entertainment ("I really enjoyed the choir today"), or self-actualization ("I don't get anything out of worship"). Our participation in the liturgy is more than a cognitive or emotional activity. Because liturgy is the "work of the people," we are called to church to do, and in doing we become. The mystery and grace of God are revealed because our needs for various types of fulfillment (educational, emotional, etc.)

are met as we "put on Christ" in the liturgy and do not make the satisfaction of those needs ends in themselves.

Matthew 5:16 has been one of the Church's traditional offertory sentences, but in recent years it has been neglected because it is so traditional. Today is a good time to use it once again and to make the point that our work in worship is a practice session for our work in the world. If liturgy is the work of the people, then all life should be liturgical, an offering to God. The Sunday liturgy is a model for the offering of the weekday liturgy. It is there that we are made salt, made light, for the zest and illumination of the world. The preacher's task is not to lay guilt on people (so easy to do with the Sermon on the Mount) because of low sodium content or brownouts, as though by our own efforts we can make life worth living. Paul's formula in today's epistle ("know nothing . . . except Jesus Christ and him crucified") can provide insight into the source of our salt and light. In our baptism we put on Christ, and in worship from week to week we are cleansed and renewed in our identity with him. Our ethical response is the sign of God's control in our lives.

Today's prayer of confession may call attention to our preference for coming to church to be served rather than being made servants. The words of forgiveness should include a clear declaration that God has made us as lights to the world who obey Jesus' Torah.

Sixth Sunday After Epiphany

Old Testament Texts

The Old Testament lessons for this Sunday articulate the completion of God's salvation and encourage the reader to enter God's new world. Deuteronomy 30:15-20 is a call for Israel to choose life in the land over death in the wilderness, while Psalm 119:1-8 provides encouragement for the worshiper, who has left the wilderness and entered the land, to persevere in walking on God's roads in God's world.

The Lesson: *Deuteronomy 30:15-20*

Bond Yourself to God and Choose Life

Setting. The book of Deuteronomy is a speech by Moses addressed to Israel as they stand on the far side of the Jordan River. These Israelites are the second generation of those who experienced the Exodus. The first generation nearly reached this same point forty years earlier but forfeited the land because they feared the risk of following God over the Jordan. The result of their lack of faith was that even though this first generation experienced God's liberation from Egypt, they were denied the land and instead were forced to wander in the wilderness—a place between the initial experience of salvation and its realization. The first generation lacked direction in their wilderness journey because they lacked faith to follow God into Canaan. Thus for them the wilderness became an endless wandering toward death. As was already noted, our lectionary text for this Sunday is one of the concluding speeches of Moses to the second generation—the children of those who died wandering. They have now reached the point where they must assess the risk of following God over the Jordan. The question that they must answer is whether the unleashing of God's power through the Exodus is reliable enough to move liberation from a wilderness experience, which is the only life that they have known, to the full-blown realization of life in the land.

Structure. Deuteronomy 30:15-20 occurs near the end of the book of Deuteronomy. It functions as a final summary or concluding exhortation to the second generation. The speech is meant to encourage these Israelites not to repeat the mistake of their parents, and instead to march ahead into the land with all the risks that such a journey might entail. As a concluding exhortation, Deuteronomy 30:15-20 picks up many of the motifs that have been structured in the book of Deuteronomy. It presents a strong conditional theology in which the singularity of faithfulness only to God is rewarded, while less risky (and thus less focused) solutions to faithfulness are punished. The text is structured around this theology of rewards and punishment in the following manner. Verse 15 provides an introduction by placing life and death before the people. Verses 16-18 fill out what the opening contrast means by presenting two conditional statements. Verse 16 offers life in the land, while vv. 17-18 sketch out the contours of a road to death. Verses 19-20 provide a conclusion to the unit by picking up the motifs of life and death from the introduction and by calling heaven and earth to witness whatever choice this second generation now makes.

Significance. Deuteronomy 30:15-20 is an exhortation to choose life. Several motifs are used to underscore what a faithful life in the land would be like: loving God, walking in God's road, keeping the law. One of the final motifs mentioned in the conclusion of the text is particularly strong, and it will provide our starting point for interpreting the others. Moses ends this little sermon by telling Israel that a choice for life requires "cleaving" to God (v. 20 RSV), or "holding fast" to God (NRSV). *Cleaving* is not a word we use frequently today. Its synonym "to cling" is probably more common, but this word in v. 20 does not mean that Israel must simply hang on tightly to God. The image goes beyond that.

Another text that uses the Hebrew word "to cleave" will aid us in interpreting Deuteronomy 30:15-20. At the end of the second creation story in Genesis 2:4-25, the writer provides us with an explanation of the mystery of marriage. This creation story is structured around the problem of finding a counterpart for the man, who does not emerge as a full character until the creation of woman. The creation of woman brings the narrative to a conclusion, with a summary by the narrator, "Therefore a man leaves his father and his mother and cleaves to his wife, and they become one flesh" (RSV). The conclusion to the second creation story illustrates how the verb *to cleave* does not mean simply to hang on tightly but to bond fundamentally. Life, for the writer of Deuteronomy, requires that we become bonded to God. With this background it is easy to see why marriage metaphors are frequently used to describe the relationship between God and the people of God. Our passage moves in a different direction by using geographical imagery to describe what it means "to cleave" to God. Cleaving to God means walking on God's road in God's land and never traveling any other roads. The map that gives us direction on this journey and marks the gas stations along the way is the law. The law is an expression of God's love, for without it we would be lost on back roads with an empty gas tank. We would wander and die in the wilderness.

The Response: *Psalm 119:1-8*

Walking on God's Road

Setting. Psalm 119:1-8 uses the same metaphors of geography and of traveling as Deuteronomy 30:15-20 to talk about the role of law in the life of faith. Note how the psalmist talks about walking in God's way (v. 3), seeking God with one's whole heart (v. 2), and observing law (v. 4). Psalm 119 is a masterful acrostic poem in which each letter of the alphabet is used for eight verses. The lectionary text for this Sunday consists of the eight lines that begin with the first letter of the Hebrew alphabet. As the primary motifs of the introductory section suggest, the psalm is probably best characterized as a hymn in praise of the law.

Structure. Psalm 119:1-8 separates into three parts. It begins in vv. 1-3 with a series of blessings directed to those who live in the world of God's law. The middle section of the psalm (vv. 4-6) addresses God directly. Note the second person pronoun in v. 4. This section divides into v. 4 and vv. 5-6. Verse 4 states that law is grounded in God and as such how it must be followed completely. Verses 5-6 shift the focus from God to the worshiper with a conditional statement, couched almost as a lament. We might paraphrase these verses "If only I could keep all of your law, then I would be a whole person (not be put to shame)." The section closes in vv. 7-8 with the psalmist rededicating his or her desire to absorb the law and, in so doing, to praise God.

Significance. You may be asking yourself, "Why all this praise of the law? As a Christian set free of the law in Christ, does it really matter?" Yes it matters. Law is essential to the Christian, and in no way should law be equated with legalism. Deuteronomy 30:15-20 has illustrated how law is really an expression of God's love. Psalm 119:1-8 is a continuation of the theology in Deuteronomy 30:15-20. Both texts are clear in their claim that law is not salvation but the result of God's salvation. God's liberating action in the Exodus, God's leading Israel through the wilderness, and God's giving of the land to Israel constitute salvation. The law is a road map of what to do once we are swept into this journey of God's. The psalmist tells us that those who stay with the map, who walk in God's way will be blessed. In praising the law, however, the psalmist is not advocating "righteousness by works."

The second and third sections of Psalm 119:1-8 make this very clear. Verses 4-6 are a conditional statement: God demands full obedience to the law (v. 4). If only the psalmist could do this (v. 5), then there would never be shame (v. 5). This section is really a lament, because it is meant to underscore how the psalmist could not possibly follow all the details of God's law, even though God commands that every law be kept diligently. The lament first gives way to renewed diligence on the part of the psalmist to absorb the law (v. 7), but ultimately it leads to a call for grace ("Do not forsake me!" v. 8), which is how the psalmist got on this road in the first place. The law is not legalism. Rather it is part of the grace of God. It is a road map of how to travel on God's roads in God's land, which eventually takes us directly through the territory of the New Testament, for Jesus is part of God's journey to the land. If we are going to follow Jesus, then God's road map is just as important as it ever was. Thus not one part, regardless of how tiny, could possibly be removed from it.

New Testament Texts

The passage from Matthew is concerned with true righteousness, while the passage from I Corinthians speaks about genuine spirituality. In different ways, both confront false claims and make assertions about the nature of authentic faith.

The Epistle: *I Corinthians 3:1-9*

Growing God's Way

Setting. Paul develops his case against the Corinthians' boasting and factionalism by using a variety of images and metaphors to correct and instruct the congregation. First, by building on the remark in 2:6 that "among the mature we do speak wisdom," he explains why he taught them no more than he did. Then, after again castigating their forming of cliques, he moves in a new direction to explain the status of Christians, especially in their relations to one another and God.

Structure. The passage for this week's reading falls into two parts. In vv. 1-4 Paul initially ties together what he had said to this point, and then he declares that the Corinthians are immature. Next, vv. 5-9 use the metaphor of a farm to explain the place of the Corinthians, Paul, and Apollos in God's household and then states God's scheme of Christian relations.

Significance. Although Paul insults the Corinthians by calling them "people of the flesh, as infants in Christ," notice that they are at least Christian babies. Paul's differences with the Corinthians do not cause the apostle to denounce the members of the congregation as sub-Christian or even non-Christian—a lesson for many zealous Christians today. By bothering to make an appeal to these people, Paul shows that he has hope for them, despite their problems. Paul's rhetoric is sharp, bordering—as it often does—on imprudence. Pastors may do well not to engage in the name-calling that the apostle does, but if the situation demands stern remarks, this passage gives precedent for a direct, even blunt, approach.

The Corinthians apparently consider themselves to be "mature," "spiritual," and even "perfect." Such parlance was common in Greco-Roman religions for describing the adherents of particular cults. Paul uses this language, probably borrowing it from the Corinthians, because it is not his manner of writing in the other epistles. He turns the words against those who claim such status. As we see in the whole letter, the Corinthians value "spiritual things" like wisdom, freedom, and perfection. But the apostle refutes their claims by saying that they could not even eat a solid Christian diet. Paul's proof of the Corinthians' immaturity is their infantile tendency toward self-centered bragging. Paul says that the Corinthians are all too human and all too little affected by the perfection of the divine. Any minister who faces a situation where the congregation is split because some members consider themselves more spiritual than others will find these verses are a powerful critique of self-centered "spirituality." In situations where one faces only nascent factionalism, the pitiful portrait of the Corinthians that Paul paints and the apostle's statements about their cliques can be used to dampen such tendencies.

In vv. 5-9 Paul takes Apollos and himself as examples to teach the Corinthians about an appropriate self-regard. Paul moves from the language of maturation to the model of a farm with its many different workers to make his points. Agriculture was a major enterprise in the Greco-Roman world. There were many large farms, owned by individuals and staffed by tens of thousands of slaves, each with a different specialization in the overall enterprise. In Paul's illustration the Corinthians would understand God to be the wealthy landholder and Paul and Apollos to be field-slaves with assignments to perform. Paul declares that the Corinthians themselves are the "field" in this metaphor. In this scheme one sees that power and authority clearly rest with God and not with any human. Moreover, it is senseless to compare people like Paul and Apollos, for though there are differences in their work, they are mere functionaries. Paul can say that he and Apollos are "fellow-workers" with God, but this is not so much a designation of status as it is an assurance that they are "on God's side." In the last part of v. 9 Paul exhausts his metaphor and turns in a new direction, saying that the Corinthians are God's "building." This remark anticipates the next metaphor about building practices and builders. In using vv. 1-9 or 5-9 for preaching and worship, one can profitably omit the shift in metaphor at the end of v. 9.

The Gospel: *Matthew 5:21-37*

Righteous Excellence

Setting. These verses continue the Sermon on the Mount. Last week's lesson (1) informed believers that we are called to be salt and light; (2) warned against inappropriate or passive living; and (3) called for obedience to God's Torah, which Jesus came to fulfill. This week we build upon the previous passage with three of six formulaic sayings that heighten Jesus' expectations concerning the Law.

Structure. The passage has four parts, which convey the practical shape of behavior and piety especially in situations of conflict. Verses 21-26 expand upon Old Testament teachings concerning murder and apply them to feeling anger toward or insulting your neighbor. Verses 27-30 expand upon the Old Testament definition of adultery; vv. 31-32 suggest that divorce may force one into adultery, and vv. 33-37 acknowledge that it is more difficult to successfully carry out an oath.

Significance. Commentators often refer to vv. 21-22 and other similarly formulated lines in the sermon as "The Antitheses" ("You have heard that it was said. . . . But I say to you. . . ."). These verses provide a specific illustration of the "fulfilling" of the Law of which Jesus speaks and to which he calls. But this line (and several of the others) does not make statements that are antithetical to the Law. Jesus shows concern for inner attitudes and motives as well as outward observable behavior.

In Exodus and Deuteronomy, adultery is defined as sexual

163

intercourse between male and female. In the Sermon on the Mount, this attempt to keep harmony in the community is expanded to preclude sexual harassment. If a man undresses a woman with his eyes, then lust is in his heart. He has committed adultery. In the hyperbolic language of the ancient Near East, adulterers are treated as common thieves, who have their offending member cut off. One who steals with a hand, loses the use of the hand; one who steals with the eye would be wise to pluck it out before losing other vital body parts!

The consequences of adultery are taken up further in vv. 31-32. In the Old Testament one finds loopholes for divorce that Matthew's church closes. Read one way Jesus removes all but one loophole—unchastity of the wife may be grounds for a certificate of divorce. Read another way, with the logic of the text, any certificate of divorce would cause the spouse to commit adultery because the spiritual covenant in a marriage can never be abrogated. Any divorce causes adultery, except in the case of unchastity, where adultery is already the state of affairs. And if a person marries a divorced person, that person has expanded the adulterous realm of relationships.

In the light of this heightening of the Torah concerning adultery, we might be tempted never to make another promise to anyone. Verses 33-36 suggest that one avoid making vows, oaths, or promises, lest he or she be accused of lying or relying upon false powers. Say yes or now, and mean it every time.

These lines have an eschatological ring, warning of judgment at several levels ("judgment," "the council," and "the hell of fire"), but Jesus actually warns about God's judgment or wrath. His caution employs stock eschatological vocabulary and stock apocalyptic eschatological images. The nature of the judgment often preoccupies preachers, but the force of Jesus' words relates to the divine character of the judgment. His point: God is concerned with human life in all its dimensions, not merely the externals or adherence to the Law.

Epiphany 6: The Celebration

Today's gospel provides a kind of scriptural warrant for placing the passing of the Peace at the conclusion of the service of the word, immediately before the presentation of the offering. Worship planners should consider using the pattern of Matthew 5:34-37, today at least, as a way of acting out liturgically the precept of our Lord. The offertory prayer should place emphasis on reconciliation as God's gift to which we respond in the offering of our gifts. For example:

> Giver of light and love:
> you enable us to be right with one another.
> May these gifts, a sign of our service
> to one another in Christ,
> help nourish the world that he died to save.
> Amen.

We have observed from the beginning of our examination of the year and its lessons that the function of the liturgy is to be understood in relation to the Paschal mystery. At no time is it more dangerous to forget that than now when the gospel lessons are from the Sermon on the Mount. The dangers on are two sides.

First, there is the danger of a neo-legalism, an emphasis on obeying the law with a Christian veneer. Christians have been given a superior law that we have to keep if Christ's atonement is to have any effect. Salvation is free after the bills are paid. Jesus himself commends the law in today's reading, and, after all, it certainly makes no sense to think that we can wander around doing whatever we like just because we are Christian. The old word for that was *antinomianism,* and the Church has frowned upon it. Christians have to try harder. That struggle makes them quite visible, so they will stand out from the rest of the world because of their ability to conform to these "kingdom standards." This sense of the law, carried to an extreme, can result in absurd situations. For example, one group of Amish that uses uncovered buggies refuses to have fellowship with another group that uses covered buggies. The reader may be able to think of other examples that are closer to home.

The other danger is to reduce Christ's teachings to ethical and moral maxims and to maintain that Christ's uniqueness is only to be found in the "higher righteousness" that he advocated. Christian living becomes a struggle to sort out motives and to "do the right thing." Charles Sheldon's novel *In His Steps*—still a big seller in many Christian bookstores—is based on this misleading understanding of Jesus' ministry.

The community needs to consider this passage christologically, because the clue to proclamation here is in the seventeenth verse, "I have come . . . to fulfill." The Christ who proclaims the excellence of the law is also the one who fulfills it for us. Even while he holds out for the Church the higher righteousness of the kingdom, it is a righteousness that he has accomplished (see the earlier commentary on the Baptism of the Lord) and that is his gift to us. We cannot fulfill it ourselves; otherwise we would not need Christ. As we meet Christ from week to week in word and sacrament, we receive the paradoxical grace of wanting to measure up and being forgiven for not having done so. Because the law of the Sermon on the Mount is a law for us, the Christian community, we dare not live without Christ.

Last Sunday After Epiphany (Transfiguration)

Old Testament Texts

This Sunday is a celebration of the Transfiguration. The Old Testament texts provide two perspectives on the presence of God in our midst. Exodus 24:12-18 describes the descent of God in the form of fire to the top of Mount Sinai in order to be with the people of God in worship, while Psalm 2:6-11 celebrates the messianic rule of God throughout this world. Taken together these texts provide commentary on the Transfiguration. (Note that Psalm 2:6-11 is the alternate reading, which is preferred in this commentary to Psalm 99, the preferred response to the lesson.)

The Lesson: *Exodus 24:12-18*

The Presence of God as Fire on the Mountain

Setting. The setting of Exodus 24:12-18 is Mount Sinai. Israel has been liberated from Egypt by God, they have passed through the water of the Red Sea and entered the wilderness, and now they have stopped at Mount Sinai as they march toward the promised land of Canaan. The setting of Mount Sinai takes over at Exodus 19 for nearly seventy-two chapters until Numbers 10. Mount Sinai is the most important setting in Israel's wilderness travels. It is so important because it is providing more information than simply a designation of geography in the wilderness. The mountain imagery is also meant to symbolize the worshiping community or more precisely how God is present in the Temple with the worshiping community. We saw how this was the case with Mount Zion (see Year A, The First Sunday of Advent), and it is now being applied to Mount Sinai. Thus the imagery of God descending to the top of Mount Sinai in Exodus 24:12-18 is really a description of how God breaks into our world through worship. As such, it is a sacramental story, or—to restate the same thing in the language of biblical studies—it is a theophanic story, a story describing how God appears to us.

Structure. Exodus 24:12-18 can be divided between vv. 12-14 and vv. 15-18. Verses 12-14 describe how Moses and Joshua were commanded by God to ascend Mount Sinai. Verses 15-18 describe the meeting of God and Moses at the mountain summit.

Significance. Verses 15-18 separate into three parts. Verse 17 is the center of this unit. It describes the appearance of the fiery glory of God before all the people of Israel. Thus the appearance of God on Mount Sinai is neither private nor esoteric. It is a public event for all people who are present at the mountain to see. Even though the focus of this text is on all the people of Israel, the entire group does not ascend the mountain to meet God. The presence of God in this world is never casual. In fact, it is always dangerous, so special persons must be chosen to represent God to the people and the people to God. Moses is that person in Exodus 24:12-18. (Though the text is ambiguous—perhaps as a result of editorial additions—Joshua is also present in an assisting role, so he is tagged as the successor to Moses.) The two parts of vv. 15-18 that frame v. 17 shift the focus from all the people of Israel to describe the movement of God (vv. 15-16) and of Moses (v. 18) on Mount Sinai. In vv. 15-16 we learn that while Moses was ascending the mountain, the glory of God was actually descending with the result that for six days Moses was simply engulfed in a cloud. The imagery here is of movement in two opposite directions—Moses ascending and God descending. After a period of preparation or purification, v. 18 concludes the unit by describing how Moses actually entered the presence of God at the summit of the mountain on the seventh day.

Exodus 24:12-18 has strong links to the creation story with the separation of six days from a special seventh day. Indeed, the links are quite intentional because priestly writers wish for us to see how our worship of God is not like the rest of our weekly activities, precisely because God is with us in a special way in the sanctuary. In the creation story of Genesis 1, note how the climax of creation is not the creation of human beings; rather, it is the celebration of Sabbath, the day God rested, which is designated as a *very* good day. In Exodus 24, the writers separate the seventh day of theophany through the repetitive motif of having Moses ascend the mountain (vv. 12, 13, 15, 18). But these ques of ascent must not mislead us from seeing the real dynamic of the story. This is not a story about ascending out of this world to meet God, but just the reverse. The central point of the story is the descent of God to the mountaintop into our world to meet Moses and to be seen by Israel. The descent of God on Mount Sinai provides the context for the extended priestly legislation that describes the construction of the tabernacle and the cult in order to allow for God to be present continually with Israel through their worship.

The Response: *Psalm 2 (Alternate Reading)*

From Worship to World

Setting. Psalm 2:1-11 is a messianic psalm or perhaps better a royal psalm that celebrates the security of both God's rule in this world and his anointed messianic king. The psalm probably functioned in a coronation ritual of the king during the monarchic period. Scholars believe that the psalm was spoken by the king in a worship setting upon ascending the throne. The language of the psalm is rooted in the confession that the power of the king rests in God and not in political might.

Structure. The boundaries of the lectionary reading may be confusing to the preacher. An outline of the entire psalm will illustrate the problems in beginning the text with v. 6. Most scholars would agree that Psalm 2 separates into four parts of roughly equal length. Verses 1-3 describe the planning of the nations. Verses 4-6 present God's reaction to the activity of the nations, in order to underscore the futility of their plans. Verses 7-9 shift from God's reaction to the nations to the divine election of the king. Finally, vv. 10-11 close the royal hymn by presenting an ultimatum to the nations to serve God. The four-part structure of the hymn could also be interpreted as presenting different speakers. Verses 1-3 present a quotation from the nations; vv. 4-6 are divine speech; vv. 7-9 are recounting by the messianic king of God's election; and vv. 10-11 are a speech by the psalmist (or perhaps the king). The four-part structure illustrates how v. 6 is a conclusion to vv. 4-5 and not an introduction to vv. 7-9.

Significance. Psalm 2 adds two points in particular to an interpretation of what the Transfiguration means for us. First, Psalm 2 provides a good counterpart to Exodus 24:12-18, because the focus on worship that was symbolized through the setting of Mount Sinai in Exodus is carried out to the very ends of the earth in the psalm. Thus, when the two texts are read together, they underscore how both worship and all aspects of this world must be transfigured because of the presence of God. Second, Psalm 2 illustrates even more poignantly a point about worship, which was made in Exodus 24:12-18: the presence of God in our world is never private or esoteric. Rather, it is a public event. In Exodus 24:12-18 the theophany of God on Mount Sinai was for all Israelites at the mountain to see. Psalm 2 takes the same argument outside the boundaries of worship and extends it to the outer reaches of our world. With its focus on all the nations, Psalm 2 illustrates how the presence of God in worship must inevitably transfigure all power structures in this world. The psalmist underscores this fact by contrasting the futile planning of the nations to overcome the heavenly rule of God. Third, Exodus 24:12-18 and Psalm 2 underscore how transfiguration is not an otherworldly experience but is about the descent of God, and that transfiguration is not complete until all aspects of our world are remade. The language of adopting the king, now the son of God (v. 7), is the psalmist's way of describing how all of reality must eventually be transfigured to the new standards that accompany God's presence in this world.

New Testament Texts

The passages from both II Peter and Matthew recount the Transfiguration of Jesus. The account in II Peter takes the point of view of an eyewitness of the event and explains the implications of that experience for inspired speaking and interpretation of scripture. Matthew's text stands back from the action and tells the story from a different point of view, that of the narrator of the gospel story, and refrains from overt interpretation or extrapolation.

The Epistle: *II Peter 1:16-21*

Eyewitnesses of His Majesty

Setting. II Peter as a whole is passionately concerned with denouncing heretical tendencies in the Church and with criticizing those engaging in "false" teaching. The letter opens in common epistolary form, naming the sender, the recipients, and issuing a greeting (vv. 1-2). Then, vv. 3-11 meditates on the significance of the believers' "call and election." In v. 12 the letter moves into a first-person style. Verses 12-15 state Peter's intentions, motivations, and purposes for writing. Our lesson continues, still in the first person, but moving to the plural, "we," and speaking as one of the eyewitnesses of the Transfiguration (vv. 16-18) in order to authenticate subsequent teaching about the value of scripture, its legitimate interpretation, and its inspiration (vv. 19-21). The subsequent sections denounce false teachers explicitly (see chapter 2).

Structure. The passage has two main parts: Verses 16-18 recount the story of the Transfiguration in language remarkably similar to the story in Matthew 17. Verses 19-21 build on this story in four moves: (1) From the experience of witnessing the Transfiguration, the apostles and, in turn, the Church "have the prophetic message more fully confirmed." Therefore, (2) believers do well to pay attention to the prophecy of scripture, (3) remembering that legitimate interpretation is not a private matter, but (4) a divinely inspired activity—apparently, from all the remarks in this letter, open to corporate critique.

Significance. This passage is concerned with the basis of legitimate Christian teaching. The opening denial that "we did not follow cleverly devised myths" differentiates the apostolic teaching about "the power and coming of our Lord Jesus Christ," done among those addressed in this letter, from teaching done by others whom II Peter identifies as false prophets (2:1). Most scholars regard II Peter as one of the latest New Testament writings—because of its apparent use of Jude and developed gospel tradition (Matthew?), its reference to the collection of Pauline letters (3:15-16), and the social setting it seems to presuppose. The mention of "cleverly devised myths" probably

171

refers to the kind of false teaching that cropped up in the Church in the mid-first century, but that developed into esoteric systems similar to pagan mystery cults late in the first century and continued well into and the second century. In such teaching, scripture was the point of departure for developing elaborate cosmological schemes and bizarre practices that were made known only to the privileged initiates of elitist circles. Today, much of what passes for "Bible study" on cable television and in the popular religious press is closer to the old "cleverly devised myths" than to valid exegesis. Second Peter's point is that true Christian faith and life are not based on such fabrications, but on the life of Jesus Christ and the divine revelation that came to his followers as they were in his presence. The real life of Jesus Christ, not someone's private musings and conclusions, is the foundation of our faith. Second Peter also contends that scripture is the guide to valid Christian living. But clearly scripture is not simply left to the individual for interpretation. Correct interpretation of scripture occurs as the Holy Spirit shows the meaning of the text to the interpreter, who is part of the community of faith—as is assumed by the steady use of "we" in this passage. Thus, when using this text for preaching, one should focus on the reality of Christ, the importance of scripture, and the role of the Holy Spirit in Christian thought and life; and all such reflection should be cast in the context of the community of faith.

The Gospel: *Matthew 17:1-9*

The One Who Remains

Setting. Matthew locates the crucial account of the Transfiguration toward the end of the narrative portion of the fourth section of his treatment of the ministry of Jesus. The incident is deliberately linked with the foregoing events: Peter's declaration at Caesarea Philippi (16:13-20), Jesus' prophecy of his death and Resurrection (16:21), Peter's rebuke of Jesus and Jesus' rebuke of Peter (16:22-23), and Jesus' words about the real price of discipleship (16:24-28). We see this grouping from the temporal note that opens the section at 16:13 ("Now when Jesus came . . .") and the coordinated temporal notes in 16:21 ("From that time. . . ."); 16:24 ("Then Jesus told his disciples . . ."); and 17:1 ("Six days later . . ."). This tightly sequential unit continues through 17:20. The Transfiguration stands at the heart of this section, both giving and finding meaning in relationship to the coordinated passages.

Structure. The story is a rapidly developing narrative that focuses on a series of events: Jesus takes the disciples up the mountain; he is transfigured; Moses and Elijah appear; Peter speaks; the cloud comes and the voice speaks; the disciples are awestruck; Jesus reassures them; Jesus and the disciples descend the mountain and he charges them to silence. The heart of the story is Jesus' transfiguration, to which all the other events relate; yet we find whatever meaning we discern for the Transfiguration as we ponder it in terms of the ancillary narrative incidents.

Significance. Scholars debate whether this story is a "misplaced post-Resurrection account," retrojected by the gospel writers into the time of Jesus' earthly ministry. Such an explanation is merely an attempt at historical rationalizing and ultimately causes us to miss the profundity of the story. George Arthur Buttrick once said, "For myself, I have never dared preach on The Transfiguration: it is the Shekinah of the New Testament. I shield my eyes and bow my head: this is a split in history. Almost the whole plan is seen in shadowed light." Indeed, Matthew's careful crafting of this narrative connotes the span of God's saving work: The story has a rich Moses typology; it takes up the heritage of Israel's scripture; it recalls Jesus' baptism; and it anticipates the cross, the Resurrection, and the Parousia.

The opening words, "Six days later," recalls the theophany at Sinai in Exodus 24—especially in relation to the ascent of a mountain where a visible transformation occurs, a cloud appears, and the voice of God is heard. In Exodus 24:16 we read, "The glory of the LORD settled on Mount Sinai, and the cloud covered it six days; on the seventh day he called to Moses out of the cloud"; and from Exodus 34:29-30 we learn that "the skin of his [Moses'] face shone because he had been talking with God."

In Matthew's telling of this story, the active hand of God is recognized subtly through the simple use of a passive verb, "he was transfigured." And while Matthew points to the glory of Jesus and the

173

respect of the disciples, he heightens the divine elements of the story (the cloud itself is "bright") as he plays down the human limitations. Unlike Mark, Matthew does not say Peter spoke in ignorance. Thus we see a strong theological bent in this narrative, as well as a rich Christology and ecclesiology, through focusing on the disciples' reverence.

Matthew emphasizes other of his major concerns in this passage. (1) The mountain motif, already seen in the Sermon on the Mount and repeated at the close of the Gospel, finds special play here as Matthew agrees with Mark (against Luke) in describing the mountain as being "high." (2) The mention of "Moses and Elijah"—rather than "Elijah and Moses," in agreement with Luke (against Mark) probably sounds one of Matthew's favorite themes: the Law and the prophets, of which Jesus is the fulfillment. (3) The voice from the cloud reiterates the words spoken at the baptism, but now there is an addition, "Listen to him!," which recognizes the authoritative nature of Jesus' teaching. (4) When the disciples fall prostrate in pious awe of the events, Matthew alone tells us that "Jesus came and touched them, saying, 'Get up and do not be afraid.' " His comforting presence and words anticipate the promise of the risen Lord, "And remember, I am with you always . . . ," showing Jesus himself to be the sole source of believers' security—"they saw no one except Jesus himself alone." We recall the angelic name for Jesus, "Emmanuel," meaning "God with us," given in the birth narrative, as well as the Gospel's closing promise.

Jesus' charge to silence employs the apocalyptic designation "the Son of Man." Whatever the historical roots of this title—either in the life of Israel or the life of Jesus—Matthew's use of the name is deliberate in the Gospel. In addition to employing this expression in the context of the Transfiguration, Matthew has Jesus speak of "the Son of Man" in relation to his death, Resurrection, and Parousia. Traditionally "the Son of Man" was God's agent for final judgment, so through these references we are to understand that in the Transfiguration, death, Resurrection, and Parousia of Jesus Christ, God is at work "to serve, and to give his life a ransom for many" (20:28).

Transfiguration: The Celebration

Transfiguration Sunday is always the Last Sunday After Epiphany, regardless of how many Sundays that may be. It provides the transition to the observance of Lent, which begins the following Wednesday. The precise function it will play for the preacher will vary from year to year under the influence of the controlling gospel. In Year A, under the influence of Matthew, the emphasis is on Jesus as successor to Moses and inaugurator of the new Israel. This is reinforced by the Old Testament lesson with its narrative of Moses going up Sinai, and the shared images of the cloud, the glory, and the voice of God.

Today's gospel takes us back to the First Sunday After Epiphany, the Baptist of the Lord, because of the occurrence of the voice confirming the identity of Jesus. At the baptism it is not made clear if onlookers hear the voice. The additional exhortation, "listen to him," in today's narrative suggests that the theophany had been for Jesus alone at the baptism, and now it is extended to selected disciples who are forbidden to tell what they have seen until after the Resurrection (v. 9). This moment of glory can only be understood in terms of the greater glory of the Resurrection, but the Crucifixion stands between as the interpretive hinge.

For churches that will celebrate the Eucharist on this day, either of the two following excerpts from the Sacramentary may serve for the christological portion of the Great Thanksgiving:

On your holy mountain he revealed himself in glory
  in the presence of his disciples.
He had already prepared them for his approaching death.
He wanted to teach them through the Law and the
Prophets that the promised Christ had first to suffer
and so come to the glory of his resurrection.

He revealed his glory to the disciples
  to strengthen them for the scandal of the cross.
His glory shone from a body like our own,
  to show that the church,
  which is the body of Christ,
  would one day share his glory.

While we should not make the mistake of the disciples and want to stay on the mountain, we should not, on the other hand, be in such haste to get back down in the valley "to heal these hearts of pain" that we end up proclaiming a salvation that is divorced from Christology.

Scripture Index

Old Testament

Apocrypha

New Testament

180

A Comparison of Major Lectionaries

YEAR A: ADVENT SUNDAY THROUGH THE LAST SUNDAY AFTER THE EPIPHANY

	Old Testament	Psalm	Epistle	Gospel
	THE FIRST SUNDAY OF ADVENT			
RCL	Isa. 2:1-5	122	Rom. 13:11-14	Matt. 24:36-44
RoCath				Matt. 24:37-44
Episcopal			Rom. 13:8-14	Matt. 24:37-44
Lutheran				Matt. 24:37-44
				or 21:1-11
	THE SECOND SUNDAY OF ADVENT			
RCL	Isa. 11:1-10	72:1-8, 18-19	Rom. 15:4-13	Matt. 3:1-12
RoCath			Rom. 15:4-9	
Episcopal				
Lutheran				

	Old Testament	Psalm	Epistle	Gospel
		THE THIRD SUNDAY OF ADVENT		
RCL	Isa. 35:1-10	146:5-10	James 5:7-10	Matt. 11:2-11
RoCath	Isa. 35:1-6, 10			
Episcopal		146		
Lutheran		146		
		THE FOURTH SUNDAY OF ADVENT		
RCL	Isa. 7:10-16	80:1-7, 17-19	Rom. 1:1-7	Matt. 1:18-25
RoCath	Isa. 7:10-14			Matt. 1:18-24
Episcopal	Isa. 7:10-17			
Lutheran	Isa. 7:10-17			
		FIRST SERVICE OF CHRISTMAS		
		(Christmas Eve or Christmas Day)		
RCL	Isa. 9:2-7	96	Titus 2:11-14	Luke 2:1-20
RoCath	Isa. 9:1-6			Luke 2:1-14
Episcopal	Isa. 9:2-4, 6-7			
Lutheran				

	Old Testament	Psalm	Epistle	Gospel

THE FIRST SUNDAY AFTER CHRISTMAS DAY

	Old Testament	Psalm	Epistle	Gospel
RCL	Isa. 63:7-9	148	Heb. 2:10-18	Matt. 2:13-23
RoCath	Sir. 3:2-6, 12-14	128:1-5	Col. 3:12-21	
Episcopal	Isa. 61:10–62:3	147	Gal. 3:23-25; 4:4-7	John 1:1-18
Lutheran		111	Gal. 4:4-7	

THE SECOND SUNDAY AFTER CHRISTMAS DAY

	Old Testament	Psalm	Epistle	Gospel
RCL	Jer. 31:7-14	147:12-20	Eph. 1:3-14	John 1:(1-9) 10-18
RoCath	Sir. 24:1-4, 8-12			
Episcopal			Eph. 1:3-6, 15-19a	Matt. 2:13-15, 19-23 or Matt. 2:1-12 or Luke 2:41-52
Lutheran	Isa. 61:10–62:3			

THE BAPTISM OF THE LORD
(The First Sunday After Epiphany)

	Old Testament	Psalm	Epistle	Gospel
RCL	Isa. 42:1-9	29	Acts 10:34-43	Matt. 3:13-17
RoCath	Isa. 42:1-4, 6-7		Acts 10:34-38	
Episcopal		89:1-29	Acts 10:34-38	
Lutheran	Isa. 42:1-7	45:7-9	Acts 10:34-38	

	Old Testament	Psalm	Epistle	Gospel
	THE SECOND SUNDAY AFTER EPIPHANY			
RCL	Isa. 49:1-7	40:1-11	1 Cor. 1:1-9	John 1:29-42
RoCath	Isa. 49:3, 5-6		1 Cor. 1:1-3	
Episcopal				John 1:29-41
Lutheran	Isa. 49:1-6	40:1-12		John 1:29-41
	THE THIRD SUNDAY AFTER EPIPHANY			
RCL	Isa. 9:1-4	27:1, 4-9	1 Cor. 1:10-17	Matt. 4:12-23
RoCath	Isa. 8:23—9:3	27:1, 4, 13-14	1 Cor. 1:10-13, 17	
Episcopal	Amos 3:1-8	139:1-17		
Lutheran	Isa. 9:1b-4 or Amos 3:1-8	27:1-9		
	THE FOURTH SUNDAY AFTER EPIPHANY			
RCL	Micah 6:1-8	15	1 Cor. 1:18-31	Matt. 5:1-12
RoCath	Zeph. 2:3; 3:12-13	146:6-10	1 Cor. 1:26-31	
Episcopal		37:1-18		
Lutheran		1	1 Cor. 1:26-31	

	Old Testament	Psalm	Epistle	Gospel
THE FIFTH SUNDAY AFTER EPIPHANY				
RCL	Isa. 58:1-9a (9b-12)	112:1-9 (10)	1 Cor. 2:1-12 (13-16)	Matt. 5:13-20
RoCath	Isa. 58:7-10		1 Cor. 2:1-5	
Episcopal	Hab. 3:1-6, 17-19	27		
Lutheran	Isa. 58:5-9a	112	1 Cor. 2:1-5	
THE SIXTH SUNDAY AFTER EPIPHANY				
RCL	Deut. 30:15-20	119:1-8	1 Cor. 3:1-9	Matt. 5:21-37
RoCath	Sir. 15:15-20	119:1-2, 4-5, 17-18, 33-34	1 Cor. 2:6-10	Matt. 5:17-37
Episcopal	Sir. 15:11-20	119:1-16		Matt. 5:21-24, 27-30, 33-37
Lutheran		119:1-16	1 Cor. 2:6-13	Matt. 5:20-37

THE TRANSFIGURATION OF THE LORD
(The Last Sunday after Epiphany)

	Old Testament	Psalm	Epistle	Gospel
RCL	Exod. 24:12-18	2:1-11 (or 99)	2 Pet. 1:16-21	Matt. 17:1-9
RoCath	The Roman Catholic Church observes the Transfiguration on the Second Sunday in Lent. Today it continues to use the sequence of proper lessons for ordinary time.			
Episcopal		99	Phil. 3:7-14	
Lutheran	Exod. 24:12, 15-18	2:6-13		

A Liturgical Calendar

Advent Through Epiphany 1992–2001

	1992–93 A	1993–94 B	1994–95 C	1995–96 A	1996–97 B
Advent 1	Nov. 29	Nov. 28	Nov. 27	Dec. 3	Dec. 1
Advent 2	Dec. 6	Dec. 5	Dec. 4	Dec. 10	Dec. 8
Advent 3	Dec. 13	Dec. 12	Dec. 11	Dec. 17	Dec. 15
Advent 4	Dec. 20	Dec. 19	Dec. 18	Dec. 24	Dec. 22
Christmas 1	Dec. 27	Dec. 26	Jan. 1	Dec. 31	Dec. 29
Christmas 2	Jan. 3	Jan. 2	------	------	Jan. 5
Epiphany 1	Jan. 10	Jan. 9	Jan. 8	Jan. 7	Jan. 12
Epiphany 2	Jan. 17	Jan. 16	Jan. 15	Jan. 14	Jan. 19
Epiphany 3	Jan. 24	Jan. 23	Jan. 22	Jan. 21	Jan. 26
Epiphany 4	Jan. 31	Jan. 30	Jan. 29	Jan. 28	Feb. 2
Epiphany 5	Feb. 7	Feb. 6	Feb. 5	Feb. 4	------
Epiphany 6	Feb. 14	------	Feb. 12	Feb. 11	------
Epiphany 7	------	------	Feb. 19	------	------
Epiphany 8	------	------	------	------	------
Last Sunday	Feb. 21	Feb. 13	Feb. 26	Feb. 18	Feb. 9

	1997–98 C	1998–99 A	1999–2000 B	2000–01 C
Advent 1	Nov. 30	Nov. 29	Nov. 28	Dec. 3
Advent 2	Dec. 7	Dec. 6	Dec. 5	Dec. 10
Advent 3	Dec. 14	Dec. 13	Dec. 12	Dec. 17
Advent 4	Dec. 21	Dec. 20	Dec. 19	Dec. 24
Christmas 1	Dec. 28	Dec. 27	Dec. 26	Dec. 31
Christmas 2	Jan. 4	Jan. 3	Jan. 2	------
Epiphany 1	Jan. 11	Jan. 10	Jan. 9	Jan. 7
Epiphany 2	Jan. 18	Jan. 17	Jan. 16	Jan. 14
Epiphany 3	Jan. 25	Jan. 24	Jan. 23	Jan. 21
Epiphany 4	Feb. 1	Jan. 31	Jan. 30	Jan. 28
Epiphany 5	Feb. 8	Feb. 7	Feb. 6	Feb. 4
Epiphany 6	Feb. 15	------	Feb. 13	Feb. 11
Epiphany 7	------	------	Feb. 20	Feb. 18
Epiphany 8	------	------	Feb. 27	------
Last Sunday	Feb. 22	Feb. 14	Mar. 5	Feb. 25